STUDIES IN ENGLISH

STUDIES IN ENGLISH

BY MEMBERS OF

UNIVERSITY COLLEGE
TORONTO

COLLECTED BY

PRINCIPAL MALCOLM W. WALLACE

———

KENNIKAT PRESS, INC./PORT WASHINGTON, N. Y.

STUDIES IN ENGLISH

First published 1931
Reissued 1969 by Kennikat Press

Library of Congress Catalog Card No: 68-26286
Manufactured in the United States of America

To

W. J. ALEXANDER

PROFESSOR OF ENGLISH LITERATURE

UNIVERSITY COLLEGE
TORONTO

1889-1926

CONTENTS

SWIFT'S VIEW OF POETRY

Herbert Davis

IT is strange that Swift has not been given more attention both on account of what he has written in verse and of what he has written about poetry. For although he did not profess to be either a poet or a critic of poetry, he is nevertheless in his casual and contemptuous manner the most extreme example that we have ever had in England of reaction against the heroic or romantic view of the poet's function and art.[1]

Dryden of course is rightly regarded as in theory and practice the great champion of the new poetry of his day, the character of which had been sketched so admirably— as we are reminded in Dr. Mark van Doren's study, *John Dryden* (1920)—in the introductory matter contributed by Waller, Denham, Hobbes, and Davenant to the latter's *Gondibert*, published in 1651. Yet Dryden never accepted fully the logical conclusion of these theories. "He spoke often, in common with his contemporaries, of the *furor*

---

[1]Perhaps this is the reason why none of Swift's editors have ever taken the trouble to provide us with an accurate text of his Poems, or even to annotate or index them properly. It is a very considerable task; and it is fortunate that it has now been undertaken by Mr. Harold Williams, who has an edition in preparation, which will be published by the *Oxford University Press*.

For convenience, I have quoted throughout this article—with page references—from the text given in the Aldine edition of the *Poetical Works* (3 vols., 1866); from the *Prose Works*, edited by Temple Scott (12 vols., 1905); and from the *Correspondence*, edited by F. Elrington Ball (6 vols., 1910-14). I have also made use of Dr. Elrington Ball's *Swift's Verse* (1929), the only book to attempt a careful and detailed study of the many critical and bibliographical problems presented by this subject.

poeticus; he championed poetic license; and he tried to write like Shakespeare." Indeed throughout his whole career Dryden continued constantly to use the traditional language whenever he spoke of the art of poetry. He remained essentially a heroic poet, and loved to flaunt the pomp and colours of his cause:

> O gracious God! how far have we
> Profan'd thy heav'nly gift of poesy!
> Made prostitute and profligate the Muse,
> Debas'd to each obscene and impious use,
> Whose harmony was first ordain'd above
> For tongues of angels, and for hymns of love!

This *Ode to Mrs. Anne Killigrew* was probably written in 1685, but again in the epistle prefixed to *Beauty in Distress* (1698), *To my Friend Mr. Motteux* he speaks of

> That sacred art, by heav'n itself infus'd
> Which Moses, David, Solomon have us'd,

And however little Dryden may have really believed in thus ascribing to the art of poetry all the sacredness that Milton had claimed for it,—at least in its finest manifestations—he would probably have readily accepted that noble claim made by Sir William Temple in his *Essay on Heroick Virtue* (1690):

"Among all the Endowments of Nature, or Improvements of Art wherein Men have excelled and distinguished themselves most in the World, there are Two only that have had the Honour of being called Divine, and of giving that Esteem or Appellation to such as possessed them in very

eminent Degrees; which are, Heroick Virtue, and Poetry:
For Prophecy cannot be esteemed any Excellency of
Nature or of Art, but, wherever it is true, is an immediate
Gift of God, and bestowed according to his Pleasure, and
upon Subjects of the meanest Capacity; upon Women or
Children, or even Things inanimate; . . . ." (*Works*, London,
1740. i, 191.)

This careful distinction here made in the use of the word
"divine" as applied to the inspiration of the poet and the
prophet respectively should be remarked. It seems to
have been preserved in the eighteenth century, so that,
while the Deists and the sceptics were making an increasingly violent attack upon the idea of the supernatural
revelation of the prophet, there was on the other hand an
almost dogmatic insistence on the true faith and the
efficacy of the canonical books, *i.e.*, the classics, in the
tradition of poetry.

This is exactly the attitude of Pope. In his attempt to
"trace for English readers the just boundaries of taste in
literature" in his *Essay on Criticism*, he shows the mentality
of a young priest of the strictest orthodoxy, bold, proud,
dogmatic, with nothing but scorn for those who are not
of the true faith. He looks upon poetry as the special
activity of a privileged and well-trained hierarchy, which
professes and believes literally in a creed that has been
handed down by the great founders and leaders of the
order. They alone have the true faith—to them the revelation has been made of Nature, "the source, and end, and
test of art."

> Those Rules of old discovered, not devis'd
> Are Nature still, but Nature methodiz'd:

Virgil found that "Nature and Homer were the same"—

> Learn hence for ancient rules a just esteem;
> To copy Nature is to copy them.

He knows himself to be a faithful member of this true church, devoted to the work to which he has been called, delighting to do honour to the great fathers of the church, who are infallible:

> Nor is it Homer nods, but we that dream.

With fine rhetoric, and not without a flash of pride, he breaks out into a great hymn in honour of the temple of poetry, and the altars of the dead still green with bays:

> Still green with bays each ancient Altar stands,
> Above the reach of sacrilegious hands;
> Secure from Flames, from Envy's fiercer rage,
> Destructive War, and all-involving Age.
> See, from each clime the learn'd their incense bring!
> Hear, in all tongues consenting Paeans ring!
> In praise so just let ev'ry voice be join'd,
> And fill the gen'ral chorus of mankind.

and himself approaches humbly to take of the fire from off the altar, that he may go forth to speak a word to the people, and declare to them the glories they can admire but not share.

> Oh may some spark of your celestial fire,
> The last, the meanest of your sons inspire,
> (That on weak wings, from far, pursues your flights;
> Glows while he reads, but trembles as he writes)
> To teach vain Wits a science little known,
> T' admire superior sense, and doubt their own!

He has all the rigour and the sternness of the true priest;
he would proscribe all field-preachers and nonconformists,
and he would stamp out every heresy. He is careful to
show that he is no sectarian, but a member of the true
church, which is limited to no small corner of the earth,
nor to a single generation, and he protests against those
who would apply "wit"

> To one small sect, and all are damn'd beside.
> Meanly they seek the blessing to confine
> And force the sun but on a part to shine,
> Which not alone the southern wit sublimes
> But ripens spirits in cold northern climes.

It is important to notice too his claim that so long as the
poet belongs to the true lineage he may receive inspiration
in many diverse ways. He does not receive his great gifts
by any mechanical operation—by a mere following of
Rules:

> Some beauties yet no Precepts can declare,
> For there's a happiness as well as care.
>
> .   .   .   .
>
> Thus Pegasus, a nearer way to take,
> May boldly deviate from the common track;
> And snatch a grace beyond the reach of art,
> Which without passing thro' the judgment, gains
> The heart, and all its end at once attains.

Thus confidently, in spite of his youth and inexperience did
Pope come forward, clothed already in the dignity and
authority of his high calling, to preach to his generation,
to saints and sinners alike, to noble lords like Lansdowne
and the Duke of Buckingham as well as outsiders like

Dennis, what he believed to be the true nature and function of poetry.

* * *

Swift had none of this professional pride, and never showed the least inclination to set much value on the business of writing poetry. He was willing to use it either to gain a reputation and establish his influence or to force his views upon the public. He wrote always not as an artist but as a man of action, or else he wrote as a gentleman writes, to amuse himself and his friends. He refused to be considered as a writer or a poet professionally. "I do not call him a poet that writes for his diversion, any more than that gentleman a fiddler, who amuses himself with a violin", he remarks in his *Letter of Advice to a Young Poet*. And he emphasizes the difference even more contemptuously, in *Thoughts on Various Subjects continued, 1726.* "A copy of verses kept in the cabinet, and only shewn to a few friends, is like a virgin much sought after and admired; but when printed and published, is like a common whore, whom anybody may purchase for half-a-crown."

This may sound like the common affectation of an eighteenth century gentleman, who was rather expected to sneer at those who fiddle for pay, or write a prologue or a dedication for ten pound. But yet it would be a greater affectation still for the author of *A Tale of a Tub* to allow himself to be impressed by such idle fancies as the poet's claim to divine honours. Is it likely that the satirist of kings and courts, politicians and lawyers, scholars and scientists, will show respect before the less tangible dignity of a poet, however magnificently he may wrap his singing robes around him? In Bedlam he had found the poets so numerous and in such poor company, that they were not worth special mention: "I shall not descend so minutely, as to insist upon the vast number of beaux, fiddlers, poets and politicians, that the world might recover. . . ."

One of the main themes of *A Tale of a Tub* is of course an analysis of "enthusiasm", which is defined as a "lifting-up of the soul, or its faculties, above matter". And in the *Discourse on the Mechanical Operation of the Spirit* he adds a fantastic travesty of a mechanistic theory of the activity of the brain, which purports to be an explanation of the way in which poetry is written. The brain is to be considered as a crowd of little animals clinging together like bees in a perpetual swarm upon a tree; "and all invention is formed by the morsure of two or more of these animals, upon certain capillary nerves, which proceed from thence, whereof three branches spread into the tongue, and two into the right hand. . . . Farther, that nothing less than a violent heat can disentangle these creatures from their hamated station of life, or give them vigour and humour to imprint the marks of their little teeth. That if the morsure be hexagonal, it produces Poetry; . . . ." (i, 201.) But perhaps the most fundamental attack upon "inspiration", which may be equally applied to the prophetical or poetical variety, is found in the preceding paragraph:

"For, I think, it is in life as in tragedy, where, it is held a conviction of great defect, both in order and invention, to interpose the assistance of preternatural power, without an absolute and last necessity. However, it is a sketch of human vanity, for every individual to imagine the whole universe is interested in his meanest concern. . . . Who, that sees a little paltry mortal, droning, and dreaming, and drivelling to a multitude, can think it agreeable to common good sense, that either Heaven or Hell should be put to the trouble of influence or inspection, upon what he is about? Therefore I am resolved immediately to weed this error out of mankind, by making it clear, that this mystery of vending spiritual gifts is nothing but a trade, acquired by as much instruction, and mastered by equal practice and application, as others are."

This attack is continued, and more specifically directed against the heroic and romantic view of poetry, in the *Letter of Advice to a young Poet* (1720). It almost takes the form of a reply to Sir Philip Sidney's "*Defence of Poesie*", as it was generally called owing to the use of this title in the numerous seventeenth century editions, in which it was printed together with the *Arcadia*. Swift appears to have the volume before him as he writes, for he refers to it constantly, sometimes with full quotation. He could easily prove, he says ironically, that

"it is impossible to be a good soldier, divine, or lawyer, or even so much as an eminent bellman, or ballad-singer, without some taste of poetry, and a competent skill in versification. But I say the less of this, because the renowned Sir Philip Sidney has exhausted the subject before me, in his "Defence of Poesie", on which I shall make no other remark but this, that he argues there as if he really believed himself." (xi, 93.)

As for the sacredness of the poet's office, suggested in such lines as these, addressed "to Spenser, in a pretended vision.

—with hands laid on, ordain me fit
For the great cure and ministry of wit.

. . . making (but reasonable) allowances for the small circumstance of profaneness, bordering close upon blasphemy,
it is inimitably fine. . . . And indeed, as of old poets and
priests were one and the same function, the alliance of
those ministerial offices is to this day happily maintained
in the same persons; and this I take to be the only justi-
fiable reason for that appellation which they so much
affect, I mean the modest title of divine poets. However,
having never been present at the ceremony of ordaining
to the priesthood of poetry, I own I have no notion of the
thing, and shall say the less of it here."

If he had needed support in thus challenging such a renowned authority Swift might well have quoted Hobbes,
who in his *Answer to Sr Will. D'Avenant's Preface Before
Gondibert* (1650) had approved of his innovation in omitting
"to invoke a Muse or some other Deity", for though he
refuses to condemn that Heathen custom in them, yet

"why a Christian should think it an ornament to his Poem,
either to profane the true God or invoke a false one, I can
imagin no cause but a reasonless imitation of Custom, of a
foolish custome, by which a man, enabled to speak wisely
from the principles of nature and his own meditation, loves
rather to be thought to speak by inspiration, like a Bagpipe.
   Time and Education begets experience; Experience
begets memory; Memory begets Judgment and Fancy:
Judgment begets the strength and structure, and Fancy
begets the ornaments of a Poem." (*Critical Essays of the
17th Century*, ed. Spingarn, ii, 59.)

There, at any rate, is an intelligent explanation of the phenomenon of poetry, which Swift may well have accepted; he would at least have approved of Hobbes' point of view. It might even be said that with all its limitations it is nevertheless sufficient to account for that kind of poetry which Swift himself produced. "Fancy begets the ornaments of a poem"—that does not go very far in explaining the particular qualities of poetry, and Hobbes would doubtless have approved of Swift's scoffing, when he comes to Sidney's claim that the essential life of poetry is found in the music of the verse:—

"the same ever honoured knight, with so musical an ear, had that veneration for the tunableness and chiming of verse, that he speaks of a poet as one that has the 'reverend title of a rhymer.'

Wherefore, you are ever to try a good poem as you would a sound pipkin, and if it rings well upon the knuckle, be sure there is no flaw in it."

What then is the real function of poetry? What justification has the young poet for obtaining a place in the kingdom? Swift answers these questions in the latter part of his letter, in which he makes definite proposals—first, "that some private street, or blind alley of this town, may be fitted up at the charge of the public, as an apartment for the Muses (like those at Rome and Amsterdam for their female relations), and be wholly consigned to the uses of our wits"—and secondly "that it might be proper to erect a corporation of poets in this city". This would provide a sort of drain to carry off the necessary purgings of the human brain, and might possibly do something to clear the corrupted air and thick fogs which are a menace to the health of the public. The letter might perhaps be regarded as a Swiftean parody of the last sentences of Temple's Essay *Of Poetry*, where he concludes that as long as the World lasts there will always be some who will be happy and content to enjoy the innocent Entertainments of music and poetry rather "than trouble the World or other Men, because they cannot be quiet themselves, though no Body hurts them".

Swift amused himself again in this year (1720) in similar fashion in verse, by laughing at the exalted flights of Grub Street wits, when sufficiently freed from the "Incumbrances of Food and Clothes", but whose inspiration immediately flags as soon as they have received their pay. It is a short poem in very colloquial octosyllabic lines, called *The Progress of Poetry* (i, 145). But it was followed much later by one of Swift's most vigorous and sustained efforts in verse, which he is said to have regarded as one of his best pieces, *On Poetry: A Rhapsody* (ii, 62), which was published anonymously in London on December 31, 1733.

Swift begins by looking over the whole commonwealth of letters, and ridiculing the strange ambition of the human race, which drives every fool to try to be a wit and a poet:

> But man we find the only creature
> Who, led by Folly, combats Nature;
> Who, when she loudly cries, Forbear,
> With obstinacy fixes there:
> And, where his genius least inclines,
> Absurdly bends his whole designs.

It is a strange and inexplicable malady, for nothing is more certain to ruin a man's chance of success than a career which offers only one single prize—the Laureate's pittance of just "one annual hundred pound".

> Not beggar's brat on bulk begot;
> Not bastard of a pedlar Scot;
> Not boy brought up to cleaning shoes,
> The spawn of Bridewell or the stews;
> Not infants dropp'd, the spurious pledges
> Of gipsies litter'd under hedges;
> Are so disqualified by fate
> To rise in church, or law, or state,
> As he whom Phoebus in his ire
> Has blasted with poetic fire.

In an earlier and happier time perhaps a Congreve or an Addison could win his way to fame and success with a poem, but now the only profitable game is to sell yourself to a corrupt and venal court—

> From party merit seek support;
> The vilest verse thrives best at court.
> A pamphlet in Sir Bob's defence
> Will never fail to bring in pence:
> Nor be concern'd about the sale,
> He pays his workmen on the nail.

Such then is the poet's fate: neither profit nor dignity nor pleasure can be found in the pursuit of poetical fame. In the world of letters, as everywhere else in life, Hobbes' view is justified that every creature lives in a state of war by nature, only here it is the lesser who prey upon the greater—a condition of things found in nature only among vermin.

> So, naturalists observe, a flea
> Has smaller fleas that on him prey;
> And these have smaller still to bite 'em,
> And so proceed *ad infinitum*.

This play of fancy in verse is simply an elaboration of the famous comment with which the king of Brobdingnag finally summed up his impressions of Gulliver's countrymen, as "the most pernicious race of little odious vermin that nature ever suffered to crawl upon the surface of the earth".

Swift is of course not concerned in this poem with any poetic ideal; he is satirising directly the inhabitants of Grub-Street, and the conditions of society which make such a Grub-Street possible.

> In bulk there are not more degrees
> From elephants to mites in cheese,
> Than what a curious eye may trace
> In creatures of the rhyming race.
> From bad to worse, and worse they fall;
> But who can reach the worst of all?
> For though, in nature, depth and height
> Are equally held infinite:
> In poetry, the height we know;
> 'Tis only infinite below.

In such a world what room is there for the sublime and the pathetic? There is nothing left to do but to rail, or simply to amuse oneself and one's friends. Swift was not one of those who could build a little private palace of art for himself, or find consolation in dreams of a better existence than the present; he was never willing to buy happiness at the price of being well-deceived, nor would he allow himself to be lulled into contentment by the soothing incantations or divine raptures of romantic poetry.

*   *   *

It would be easy of course to suggest that just as Swift's satire on politicians was largely due to his bitter hatred of Walpole and the Whigs, and his fall with the Tories from power and influence, so his satire on poets was due to his early disappointments and failures, and especially to Dryden's emphatic and rather brutal judgment on his attempts to gain atttention by writing Pindaric Odes after the manner of Cowley. But Swift, however unable to forget such a remark, was hardly one to be crippled by it, and we have evidence enough to show how he came to scorn the poetic Muse, scoff at her claims for devotion, and turn his technical skill as a verse-writer to account in the service of a less romantic mistress.

Perhaps too much has been made of Swift's confession that he was devoted to Cowley's poetry while he was still at school, for he seems to have begun to write verse himself in a very different vein,—crude satirical doggerel intended to satisfy the taste of his fellow undergraduates at Trinity College. In Dr. Elrington Ball's study, *Swift's Verse*, reference is made to all the early verses attributed to Swift by Vice-Provost Barrett in his *Essay on the earlier part of the Life of Swift*, and later by Sir William Wilde on the evidence of the Christie volume—a sort of commonplace book of Swift's which dates from his undergraduate years. Whether we regard any of these verses as the work of Swift or not, perhaps more importance should be attached to the fact that here at any rate are verses which

Swift copied out in his own hand, which show already that his taste was entirely for satire and buffoonery and for occasional poems concerned with public affairs and political and religious controversy. Here is an early indication of Swift's natural bent; and this is very significant in showing that it was only after settling at Moor Park—and I suggest under the direct influence of Sir William Temple—that he turned aside and was persuaded to try to imitate Cowley, and indulge in what Dr. Ball very rightly calls a period of "Pindaric and Heroic Aberration". And a careful study of these pieces, which are not by any means as uninteresting or as weak as is often suggested, show Swift struggling with an unsuitable medium, and forced into an attitude, a pose which he soon recognized as an affectation, and then contemptuously abandoned. It is perhaps worth remarking that only the *Ode to the Athenian Society* (i, 22), was published in his lifetime. Dunton had printed it as the work of a country gentleman in the Supplement to the *Fifth Volume of the Athenian Gazette*, 1691, and it was printed again in pamphlet form in 1725 with the title— *Sphinx: A Poem ascrib'd to certain Anonymous Authors: By the Revd. Dean S—t.* The rest of these Moor Park poems were first printed by Hawkesworth in *Swift's Works*, 1755.

They are interesting because here we see Swift for the only time trying seriously to be a poet. His letters indicate that he set himself industriously to try for fame in the conventional manner following the example of Dryden and Cowley. He comes to pay his court to the accepted Muse, with panegyrics in Pindaric form. And the result is exactly what we should expect. What had he to do with writing the praise of great men, giving honour to noble deeds?

Was the world that he knew, even at that time, a place for compliments and the praise of beauty and virtue?

But it was while he was making these experiments that he began to realize how much cant there is in all this talk of the divine inspiration of the poet.

> Thus the deluding Muse oft blinds me to her ways,
> And ev'n my very thoughts transfers
> And changes all to beauty and the praise
> Of that proud tyrant sex of hers.
> The rebel Muse, alas! takes part,
> But with my own rebellious heart.

>   .   .   .   .   .   .

And in the *Ode to Archbishop Sancroft* (i, 1), written probably two years later, panegyric turns already into scepticism and satire—

> No wonder, then, we talk amiss
> Of truth, and what, or where it is;
> Say, Muse, for thou, if any, know'st,
> Since the bright essence fled, where haunts the reverend ghost?

This appeal to the Muse for guidance, with that little qualification, "thou, if any, know'st" is very like Swift.

And again:

> Forgive (original mildness) this ill-govern'd zeal,
> 'Tis all the angry slighted Muse can do
>   In the pollution of these days;
> No province now is left her but to rail,
> And poetry has lost the art to praise,
>   Alas, the occasions are so few:

Nevertheless in the *Ode to Sir William Temple* (i, 12) written about the same time, he seems determined to put aside all doubts and try what he can do. Here after an outburst in Temple's own manner against "philosophy, the lumber of the schools" and the "ill-manner'd pedantry" of those who

> . . . purchase knowledge at th' expense
> Of common breeding, common sense,
> And grow at once scholars and fools;

he devotes himself to limitless adulation of his patron, and of that quiet life in a country retreat which he has chosen, and launched in full career boasts at last of his own slavery to the poetic Muse, and even refers to the hopes and encouragements that have bound him to her service.

> Nature the hidden spark did at my birth infuse,
> And kindled first with indolence and ease;
> And since too oft debauch'd by praise,
> 'Tis now grown an incurable disease:
> In vain to quench this foolish fire I try
> In wisdom and philosophy:
> In vain all wholesome herbs I sow,
> Where nought but weeds will grow
> Whate'er I plant (like corn on barren earth)
> By an equivocal birth,
> Seeds, and runs up to poetry.

This was the end of the Pindarics, though not of complimentary verse. It is almost as though Swift realized that this was in every way the least sincere piece he ever wrote. And in the two poems that follow *To Mr. Congreve* (i, 34), and *Occasioned by Sir William Temple's late Illness and*

Recovery (i, 43), he is too much concerned with his own disillusionment to have much thought for his subjects. It is true that he talks of disappointment and despair, but I do not feel with Dr. Elrington Ball that he was despondent "because of his failure to succeed in the Cowleyan School". It is true too that for the next five years from 1693-8 he wrote no more verses—or at least none survive—but that may equally well be due to the fact that he had discovered, not that he could not write like Cowley or Dryden, but that he did not want to. There was no sign of lack of confidence surely in the famous lines:

> My hate, whose lash just Heaven has long decreed
> Shall on a day make sin and folly bleed:

nor in the lines quoted from a lost Ode, inscribed "The Poet":

> Beat not the dirty paths where vulgar feet have trod,
> But give the vigorous fancy room.
> For when, like stupid alchymists, you try
> To fix this nimble god,
> This volatile mercury,
> The subtle spirit all flies up in fume;
> Nor shall the bubbled virtuoso find
> More than a fade insipid mixture left behind.

It is hardly the voice of the disappointed worshipper, rejected by the Muse that he had patiently courted, but of one who is thoroughly disillusioned, and anxious to expose the cheat that he had detected, that we hear in such lines as these:

> Malignant goddess! bane to my repose,
> Thou universal cause of all my woes;

Say whence it comes that thou art grown of late
A poor amusement for my scorn and hate;

.   .   .   .

Ah, should I tell a secret yet unknown,
That thou ne'er hadst a being of thy own,
But a wild form dependent on the brain,
Scattering loose features o'er the optic vein;
Troubling the crystal fountain of the sight,
Which darts on poets' eyes a trembling light;
Kindled while reason sleeps, but quickly flies,
Like antic shapes in dreams, from waking eyes:
In sum, a glitt'ring voice, a painted name,
A walking vapour, like thy sister fame.

And finally, with a triumphant cry he breaks away,
turning his back upon visionary dreams and fancies, eager
only to gaze with untroubled sight upon a world of reality:

There thy enchantment broke, and from this hour
I here renounce thy visionary power;
And since thy essence on my breath depends,
Thus with a puff the whole delusion ends.

Instead of poetry Swift turned to prose satire, and in the
following years until the death of Sir William Temple, was
probably mainly occupied with the *Tale of a Tub*. When
that finally appeared in 1704, its author must have felt
that he had successfully evaded the power of the malignant
goddess, who troubles the crystal fountain of the sight, and
fills the brain with antic shapes while reason sleeps. And
if further proof was required of his emancipation, it could
scarcely have been better provided than in the volume of
Miscellanies, published in 1711, in which he included
thirteen poems, chosen out of a considerable amount of

political and satirical verse, some already published as
Broadsides. It seems almost as if he wished to flout the
votaries of the heroic and romantic muse by ostentatiously
placing at the very beginning of this little group the lines
Written in a Lady's Ivory Table-book, 1698 (i, 49). Here
instead of compliment or a lover's devotion, he makes a
collection of some of the stupidest of the senseless trifles it
contains, and exposes them as a revelation of its owner's
heart:

> Here you may read, "Dear charming saint;"
> Beneath, "A new receipt for paint:"
> Here, in beau-spelling, "Tru tel deth;"
> There, in her own, "For an el breth:"
>
> .   .   .   .
>
> Who that had wit would place it here,
> For every peeping fop to jeer?

And this is followed by the delightfully absurd chatter of
The humble petition of Frances Harris (i, 50), with its
vigorous caricatures of the servants in the Earl of Berkeley's
household. It almost seems as if immediately Swift
escaped from the restrained and dignified atmosphere of
Sir William Temple's household, where he had tried to
produce conventional poetry, and returned to Dublin in
the train of the Earl of Berkeley, he found encouragement
to indulge his own taste for ridicule and burlesque. Temple
had particularly disapproved of this in his essay on *Ancient
and Modern Learning:*—

"I wish the Vein of Ridiculing all that is Serious and Good,
all Honour and Virtue, as well as Learning and Piety, may
have no worse Effects on any other States: 'Tis the Itch of

our Age and Climate, and has over-run both the Court
and the Stage; enters a House of Lords and Commons, as
boldly as a *Coffee*-House, Debates of Council as well as
private Conversation; and I have known, in my Life, more
than one or two Ministers of State, that would rather have
said a Witty Thing, than done a Wise One; and made the
Company laugh, rather than the Kingdom rejoice."
(*Works*, London, 1740. i, 169.)

And Swift himself in the *Battle of the Books* had upheld
Temple in this, and gone on further to scoff at the characteristically modern claim for originality.

"For anything else of genuine that the Moderns may pretend to, I cannot recollect; unless it be a large vein of
wrangling and satire, much of a nature and substance with
the spider's poison; which, however they pretend to spit
wholly out of themselves, is improved by the same arts, by
feeding upon the insects and vermin of the age". (i, 172.)

This was probably written in the latter part of 1697, and
this scornful attitude towards even the genuine productions
of the Moderns was doubtless intended to win the approval
of his dignified patron. It is strange that none of Swift's
critics, so far as I know, have turned this to account, by
quoting it as a good description of a great deal of his own
writing, which is certainly—as Swift liked himself to think
—"spit wholly out of himself" and often improved "by
feeding upon the insects and vermin of the age".

*   *   *

Few of Swift's biographers and critics have indeed
troubled much with his poetry; like Dr. Johnson, they

find little upon which to exercise their powers, and are content to compliment him on his facility and ease, or protest against his outspokenness, without indicating very clearly the character and significance of his work as a whole. They often give the impression that like Lord Orrery they would have been better pleased if his editors had not been so active in bringing together every trifle that may have come from his pen. "Many of them"— he says—"are spurious, and many more are trifling, and in every respect improper for the public view;" an attitude, which is of course in accord with his pompous conventionality, shown in his remarks on the "low humour" of the *Directions to Servants:*

"Superior talents seem to have been intended by Providence as public benefits, and the person, who possesses such blessings, is certainly answerable to Heaven for those endowments, which he enjoys above the rest of mankind. Let him jest with dignity, and let him be ironical upon useful subjects: leaving poor slaves to *heat their porridge* or *drink their small beer,* in such vessels as they shall find proper. The Dean, it seems, had not this way of thinking". (*Remarks, etc.,* London, 1752. p. 180.)

He certainly had not; and it was with very different standards from those of his Lordship that Swift chose out of all the infinite variety of circumstance the particular occasion for poetry; and when the occasion demanded, he never refused the challenge, and often answered with surprising readiness and quickness. Most frequently his poetry was prompted entirely from without, as was all the political verse, and a great deal that belongs to his friendships and enmities. There is no more struggle, as in his early attempts, at heroic verse. He never courts the Muse, but turns instead to the laughing and irrepressible demon of satire, always ready at his elbow to use anything or anybody for its own disreputable purpose. It may be a mere Partridge—shoemaker, quack, and astrologer, who is given an elegy exalting him to a place among the heavenly bodies, where he may still follow his calling. Or it may be Lord Cutts—who, while acting temporarily as a Lord Justice in Ireland in 1705, was the first of many who held that office to attract Swift's violent dislike—whose character and appearance are made to fit so admirably Pliny's description of a Salamander. Or it may be a more pleasant joke, delightfully elaborated on the subject of the tiny house that Vanbrugh, the architect and dramatist, had built out of the profits of a play. Or even a street scene in the City in the early morning, or when it is raining— the two perfect sketches in heroic couplets, which Swift contributed to the *Tatler*.

It is interesting to note that the second of these—the *Description of a City Shower* (i, 93)—had, as Dr. Elrington Ball points out, "an ulterior motive, namely, to make the use of the triplet and alexandrine ridiculous", in these concluding lines:

Sweepings from butchers' stalls, dung, guts, and blood,
Drown'd puppies, stinking sprats, all drench'd in mud,
Dead cats, and turnip-tops come tumbling down the
    flood.

It has perhaps not been clearly enough recognized that a good number of Swift's pieces owe their existence entirely to such purely literary motives. However true it may be that much of his writing is the work of a man of action rather than a man of letters, yet Swift was always very closely associated with the literary world, and keenly interested in the work of his contemporaries. He was concerned moreover to influence their taste, and to do that he employed his usual method of satirizing what seemed to him to be the affectations and absurdities of poetical fashions. He scorned above all the artificial conventions, the outworn ornaments and false sentimentality, which are perhaps at all times the marks of minor poetry. There can be no better proof of the real attitude of this great Augustan towards such poetry than is afforded in two little parodies, written probably in 1733—*A Love Song in the modern Taste* (ii, 53), and an *Ode to Science* (ii, 58). All the usual tricks are here exposed—the ornamental epithet, the classical references, the personification, the alliteration, the sing-song lilt, the unreal language, the sentimental commonplaces, and all the dreary staleness of these false, imitated, poetical devices:

> Cynthia, tune harmonious numbers;
>   Fair Discretion, string the lyre;
> Sooth my ever-waking slumbers:
> Bright Apollo, lend thy choir.
>
> Melancholy smooth Meander,
>   Swiftly purling in a round,
> On thy margin lovers wander,
>   With thy flowery chaplets crown'd.

Or this more elaborate stanza, in praise of Science:

> Bid bright Astræa gild the morn,
> Or bid a hundred suns be born,
>   To hecatomb the year;

> Without thy aid, in vain the poles,
> In vain the zodiac system rolls,
> In vain the lunar sphere.

Again, in a reply to some complimentary verses by Dr. Delany, *News from Parnassus*—which reports that at a session of the poets on Parnassus, convened by Apollo on February 27, 1720, Swift was appointed his vicegerent on earth—Swift, assuming this new dignity, issues what he called *Apollo's Edict* (i, 132), and in a very easy pleasant manner proclaims therein what may and what may not be done by his vassals. Swift's own methods are of course to be imitated:

> Let his success our subjects sway,
> Our inspirations to obey,
> And follow where he leads the way;
> Then study to correct your taste;
> Nor beaten paths be longer traced.

T' en follows a list of things to be avoided—all the worn-out tags of poetic finery:

> No simile shall be begun,
> With setting or with rising sun; . . .

> No son of mine shall dare to say,
> Aurora usher'd in the day,
> Or ever name the milky-way. . . .

> Your tragic heroes shall not rant,
> Nor shepherds use poetic cant.

Even Denham's famous line so often quoted and so much admired is forbidden:

3

> Nor let my votaries show their skill
> In aping lines from Cooper's Hill;
> For know I cannot bear to hear
> The mimicry of deep, yet clear.

And especially of course he proscribes all the nonsense of love-poetry;

> When you describe a lovely girl,
> No lips of coral, teeth of pearl.
>   Cupid shall ne'er mistake another,
> However beauteous, for his mother;
> Nor shall his darts at random fly
> From magazine in Celia's eye.

A more violent attack on poetic cant is made in a little group of poems, which were included in the *Miscellanies* by Pope in 1727. The first of these—*Phyllis; or, The Progress of Love, 1716* (i, 112)—which gives the past history of the landlord and hostess of the Old Blue Boar, at Staines, which Swift used to pass on his journeys to Windsor, is possibly a version of some story he has heard; but even if that is so, it is certainly at the same time a satire upon the popular notions of romantic love and such attendant follies as a girl's elopement with a servant to escape from a reasonable match properly arranged by her parents. She leaves behind of course a note of explanation and an appeal to her father for forgiveness:

> ('Tis always done, romances tell us,
> When daughters run away with fellows)
>
> .   .   .   .
>
> It was her fate, must be forgiven;
> For marriages were made in Heaven;

His pardon begg'd: but, to be plain,
She'd do't if 'twere to do again:
Thank'd God, 'twas neither shame nor sin;
For John was come of honest kin.
Love never thinks of rich and poor;
She'd beg with John from door to door.

The adventures which befell them are very rapidly sketched, until at last

Fate put a period to the farce,
And with exact poetic justice;
For John was landlord, Phyllis hostess;
They keep, at Stains, the Old Blue Boar,
Are cat and dog, and rogue and whore.

It is worth while to compare with this poem a letter that Swift wrote to Mrs. Swanton, a distant relative, on July 12, 1733 giving her advice how to deal with her daughter who had left her home in order to be free to marry according to her own wishes.

"Although such an action in a daughter whom you have used so well can deserve no pardon, yet I would have you leave her without excuse. Send to her to come home; if she refuse, send a second and third time, and if she still refuseth, let her know in plain terms, that you will never have the least correspondence with her, and when she is ruined, as will certainly be the case, that you will never see her, nor give or leave her or her children, if she have any, a morsel of bread. Let her know you have given her fair warning, and if she will run into destruction with her eyes open, against common sense and the opinion of all rational people, she hath none to blame but herself; and that she must not expect to move your compassion some years hence with the cries of half a dozen children at your door for want of bread. . . ." (*Corr.* v, 11.)

In life and in literature Swift never ceased to protest against ideas and conduct, which he considered "against common sense and the opinion of rational people".

The Progress of Beauty, 1720 (i, 140) shows how Swift is prepared to deal himself with subjects, which have been sicklied o'er with the sentimentality of romantic poets. And I would suggest that some of the unpleasant qualities of these poems, which have caused his admirers so much difficulty, may have been due as much to his impatience with poetic cant as to any unspeakable perversions in his mind. "No lips of coral, teeth of pearl" he had already demanded; now he goes a little further, and substitutes for the usual flatteries such lines as these. Is it the beauty of the moon that the poets celebrate, then let them look more closely:

> When first Diana leaves her bed,
>   Vapours and steams her look disgrace,
> A frowsy dirty-colour'd red
>   Sits on her cloudy wrinkled face:

And there is an exact parallel between earthly females and the moon:

> To see her from her pillow rise,
>   All reeking in a cloudy steam,
> Crack'd lips, foul teeth, and gummy eyes,
>   Poor Strephon! how would he blaspheme!

It is only a matter of shifting the colours round, as he proceeds very innocently to explain:

Three colours, black, and red, and white,
  So graceful in their proper place,
Remove them to a different site,
  They form a frightful hideous face:

For instance, when the lily skips
  Into the precincts of the rose,
And takes possession of the lips,
  Leaving the purple to the nose:

So Celia went entire to bed,
  All her complexion safe and sound;
But, when she rose, white, black, and red,
  Though still in sight, had changed their ground.

The comparison is continued throughout, and Celia's
fading beauties given no longer date than the waning
moon; the last stanza closes the story with a gay little note,
unusual in Swift.

Ye powers who over love preside!
  Since mortal beauties drop so soon,
If ye would have us well supplied,
  Send us new nymphs with each new moon!

*   *   *

It may be said of course that these are all very slight
productions, and that it is not of much real significance
that Swift amuses himself thus in attacking the romantic
attitude. The test comes only when he is actually confronted by those experiences in life which have inspired
the poets with their most sublime utterances. Is there
any evidence that at such moments Swift turned to poetry?

Does he succeed then in still maintaining his complete control of himself? Is it true that he never touches "the sublime or the pathetic", is he never betrayed into sentimentality, or stirred to emotional fervour?

We should expect to find an answer in *Cadenus and Vanessa* and in the *Stella* poems which Swift allowed Pope to include in the Miscellanies in 1727. Fortunately we do not need here to repeat all the stories that have been written about the two women whom Swift loved. We are only concerned with the way in which he treats these personal experiences of love and friendship in his verse. We are concerned with the poems as literature, not as a clue to certain biographical problems, however intriguing. And *Cadenus and Vanessa* (ii, 196) is as literary as anything that Swift ever produced. Apart from the title, which alone removes it just outside the world of plain happenings, Swift has carefully framed it in a fantasy, in which gods and goddesses play their part, endowing Vanessa with graces and gifts rarely combined in women. And when this prodigy is finally introduced into the world, Swift indulges his usual banter at the expense of the "fashionable fops" and "glittering dames From around the purlieus of St. James':

> Both sexes, arm'd with guilt and spite,
> Against Vanessa's power unite:
> To copy her few nymphs aspired;
> Her virtues fewer swains admired.

But a few had better taste, whom she entertained with pleasing arts. Among these was Cadenus; and Cupid—piqued at his lack of success with her—determines to take revenge, by making her fall in love with him.

> Cadenus is a subject fit,
> Grown old in politics and wit,
> Caress'd by ministers of state,
> Of half mankind the dread and hate.

It is curious that Vanessa is represented as being particularly affected by some lines in a poem of Swift's:

> Cadenus many things had writ:
> Vanessa much esteem'd his wit,
> And call'd for his poetic works:
> Meantime the boy in secret lurks;
> And while the book was in her hand,
> The urchin from his private stand
> Took aim, and shot with all his strength
> A dart of such prodigious length,
> It pierced the feeble volume through,
> And deep transfix'd her bosom too.
> Some lines, more moving than the rest,
> Stuck to the point that pierced her breast,
> And, borne directly to the heart,
> With pains unknown increased her smart.

As the episode referred to must have taken place in 1712 or 1713, when Swift's published verses were still very slight in bulk, it is tempting to speculate what these lines could have been—unless this specific detail is merely a little joke. Most of Swift's biographers agree that it probably happened sometime after his return to London, on September 9, 1713, on one of his visits to the court at Windsor, which continued until the end of December, 1713. On October 31, Swift had addressed some lines *To Lord Harley, on his Marriage* (i, 109), and in this poem there is at least a passage which might very well have served as an introduction to Vanessa's declaration of love. For there Swift in an unusual vein of happy compliment praises Harley's young bride, the daughter of the Duke of Newcastle, for her sensible choice of the virtuous and the learned Harley, in preference to the glittering crowd of fortunes and titles that had aspired to her. How aptly, if Vanessa had been reading this poem, could she have turned the argument to her own purpose. She too had been taught by Swift to despise the ordinary ways of the world:

> Terrestrial nymphs, by formal arts,
> Display their various nets for hearts:
> Their looks are all by method set,
> When to be prude, and when coquette;
> Yet, wanting skill and power to choose,
> Their only pride is to refuse.
> But, when a goddess would bestow
> Her love on some bright youth below
> Round all the earth she casts her eyes;
> And then descending from the skies,
> Makes choice of him she fancies best, . . .

Her taste was surely even more exalted, leading her to choose before all the Court a Dean twice her age. The latter part of the poem has always been regarded as a reliable account of what happened. Naturally when the poem was published in 1726, Swift wishing to dismiss it lightly, referred to it in a letter to Knightley Chetwode, April 19, 1726, as "a task performed on a frolic among some ladies at Windsor . . . for my own part, I forget what is in it, but believe it to be only a cavalier business . . . a private humorsome thing, which, by an accident inevitable, and the baseness of particular malice, is made public." (*Corr.* iii, 306.)

That is perhaps hardly fair, and yet the phrases "a cavalier business"—"a private humorsome thing" are not inaccurate descriptions of the poem. Whatever the episode itself was—however charged with passion and pity, however difficult and dangerous—Swift treats it with as little emotion as possible; he is neither cynical nor sentimental, he detaches himself gently from it, and places it a little way off, and sees it as something separate, a private affair of Cadenus and Vanessa, a delicate subject to be touched carefully with wit and fancy and humour.

Nothing that Swift ever wrote shows more perfectly his mastery of himself and his art than these lines, describing at length the dispute between Cadenus and Vanessa. He recognizes the force of her argument, he is fairly caught, it is a "bite". But he may well be proud at her confession,

> Construing the passion she had shown,
> Much to her praise, more to his own.
> Nature in him had merit placed,
> In her, a most judicious taste.

In return he gladly offers her "friendship in its greatest height".

> His want of passion will redeem
> With gratitude, respect, esteem;
> With what devotion we bestow
> When goddesses appear below.

But Vanessa has been taught too well by him; she knows the proper value of such "exalted strains"—

> The nymph in sober words entreats
> A truce with all sublime conceits;
> For why such raptures, flights, and fancies,
> To her who durst not read romances?
> In lofty style to make replies,
> Which he had taught her to despise?

She will have her turn to be tutor, and will teach him the science

> Wherein his genius was below
> The skill of every common beau,

And now in this extremely delicate situation, how is Swift to avoid either the bathos of a happy ending, or a hint perhaps of the tragedy that was to follow. He preserves instead the "humorsome" tone perfectly, by ending in cavalier fashion—

> But what success Vanessa met,
> Is to the world a secret yet.
> Whether the nymph, to please her swain,
> Talks in a high romantic strain;
> Or whether he at last descends
> To act with less seraphic ends;
> Or to compound the business, whether
> They temper love and books together;
> Must never to mankind be told,
> Nor shall the conscious Muse unfold.

The poems to Stella are if possible both in subject and in style an even more complete triumph over any temptation to indulge in sentiment or romance; and it is surprising, as Dr. Elrington Ball remarks, "that Swift could have borne the publication of these verses, especially when

he believed her to be dying and was writing to Sheridan
in an agony of affliction". And he can only offer the not
very convincing explanation that it was due to Swift's
infatuation for Pope and his wish to leave the arrangement
of the *Miscellanies* entirely in his hands. It may well be
that Pope was anxious to have as much new material as
possible in order to give some justification for the publisher's advertisement, which described the *Last Volume*
as "consisting of several Copies of Verses, most of them
never before printed". But it is perhaps equally reasonable to suppose that Swift definitely wished to include,
and set over against the *Cadenus and Vanessa*, these plain
records of his friendship with Stella.

The Birthday Verses belong to the last years of her life,
1719-1727, and are perfectly described by a phrase which
Swift uses to describe the character of his poetry in some
lines written *To Mr. Delany, Nov. 10, 1718.* (i, 116.)

> To you the Muse this verse bestows,
> Which might as well have been in prose;
> No thought, no fancy, no sublime,
> But simple topics told in rhyme.

He might perhaps have gone further and said that he sometimes wrote verse because it was easier than to write
prose. The doggerel trifles that he tossed off in his con-
tests with Sheridan were of course very much easier:

> Because hot weather makes me lazy
> To write in metre is more easy.

and sometimes he wrote with his left hand, while the
other was engaged in other business, or (if we may believe
his time-keeping) at the tremendous speed of 38 rhyming

lines "Written, signed, and sealed, five minutes and eleven seconds after the receipt of yours, allowing seven seconds for sealing and superscribing, from my bed-side, just eleven minutes after eleven, Sept. 15, 1718". (iii, 251.) But in his best work too, Swift forces the rhymed octosyllabic couplet to serve him as a means of obtaining an effect of perfect spontaneity and ease,—a medium of expression even less formal than prose. Most poets use verse where prose would not be good enough for their particular purpose. Swift seems almost to have used it as a more familiar, more intimate way of communication. He could do anything he liked with prose—except, I think, that he was not a master of the familiar style; even in the *Journal to Stella* he is obliged to fall back upon "little language".

And so, just as in dealing with his enemies in political controversy he used verse for his roughest and least considered outbursts, tossing off ballads and broadsides shaped to popular tunes, so in his friendships his most familiar manner of address was always in verse. What could be more familiar—and at the same time an excellent parody on the usual complimentary Birthday-Odes—than the first of the poems written for *Stella's Birthday, March 13, 1718-19* (ii, 229).

> Stella this day is thirty-four,
> (We sha'n't dispute a year or more:)
> However, Stella, be not troubled,
> Although thy size and years are doubled
> Since first I saw thee at sixteen, . . .

He delights always to emphasize that she is no longer either young or beautiful—

> An angel's face a little crack'd,

he boasts that in all his addresses to her there had been
only sincerity—*To Stella, who collected and transcribed his
Poems, 1720* (ii, 232.)

> Thou, Stella, wert no longer young,
> When first for thee my harp was strung,
> Without one word of Cupid's darts,
> Of killing eyes, or bleeding hearts;
> With friendship and esteem possest,
> I ne'er admitted Love a guest.
>
> .   .   .   .   .   .
>
> Your virtues safely I commend;
> They on no accidents depend:
> Let malice look with all her eyes,
> She dares not say the poet lies.

There are a good many commonplaces, and too many
repetitions on the birthday theme, which Swift himself
seems to have tired of, for in 1724-5 he complains that he
can no longer dance in rhyme: (ii, 255.)

> Adieu! bright wit, and radiant eyes!
> You must be grave and I be wise.
> Our fate in vain we would oppose:
> But I'll be still your friend in prose:
> Esteem and friendship to express,
> Will not require poetic dress;
> And if the Muse deny her aid
> To have them sung, they may be said.

Yet two years later, on Stella's last birthday, he offers her
a splendid final poem, where without any change of tone
these plain prosaic octosyllables take on real force and
dignity. (ii, 264.)

> This day, whate'er the Fates decree,
> Shall still be kept with joy by me:
> This day then let us not be told,
> That you are sick, and I grown old;
> Nor think on our approaching ills,
> And talk of spectacles and pills;
> Tomorrow will be time enough
> To hear such mortifying stuff.

In such verses we can perhaps best feel the limitations of Swift's poetry; for here in a line or two we can see them as it were just giving way. That severe plainness of speech, that unwillingness to allow words to become emotional or musical,—the flat tonelessness of many of the serious poems almost disappears, and we are half persuaded that we can distinguish tones from another kind of poetry in that last couplet:

> Tomorrow will be time enough
> To hear such mortifying stuff.

But still he limits himself to his particular theme, and allows nothing fanciful or extraneous to enter. It was doubtless Swift himself who chose the title for the volume of poems which Faulkner included in the first collected edition of the *Works*, 1735—*Poems on several Occasions*. It is a most accurate description—for all his verse is in the strictest sense occasional, and when the occasion is private, he rarely allows it to expand into general significance. This is partly because verses like these to Stella were written primarily for her and for their friends, without any consideration of a wider audience. When the occasion is public, the poetry is often more powerful, for then it is

generally aimed with a definite purpose at the larger
public; with the result that it takes on a character which
Scott has well described:

"Sometimes, however, the intensity of the satire gives to
his poetry a character of emphatic violence, which borders
upon grandeur." It "indicates rather ardour of temper
than power of imagination. *Facit indignatio versus.* The
elevation of tone arises from the strong mood of passion
rather than from poetical fancy."

There was one great occasion which Swift took full
advantage of,—the death of the Duke of Marlborough.
The poem was *A Satirical Elegy on the death of a late
famous General, 1722* (i, 173.)

> His Grace! impossible! what, dead!
> Of old age too, and in his bed!
>
> .   .   .   .   .   .
>
> This world he cumber'd long enough;
> He burnt his candle to the snuff;
> And that's the reason, some folks think,
> He left behind so great a stink.
> Behold his funeral appears,
> Nor widows' sighs, nor orphans' tears,
> Wont at such times each heart to pierce,
> Attend the progress of his hearse.
> But what of that? his friends may say,
> He had those honours in his day.
> True to his profit and his pride,
> He made them weep before he died.
> Come hither, all ye empty things!
> Ye bubbles raised by breath of kings!
> Who float upon the tide of state;
> Come hither, and behold your fate!

> Let Pride be taught by this rebuke,
> How very mean a thing's a duke;
> From all his ill-got honours flung,
> Turn'd to that dirt from whence he sprung.

Is truth, or prejudice, too nakedly exposed? Must we therefore say that this cannot be poetry? If the imagination may trace the noble dust of Alexander till it is found stopping a bung-hole, may it not also triumph in the return of the ignoble to "that dirt from whence he sprung"?

Swift seems to delight to go through the whole realm of poetry, turning everything upside down. If we look for elegies, fitting a solemn moment, this is what we find; if we want sentiment and the delicate play of fancy, we are offered a parody of Cowley's *Clad all in White*—one of the Love-Verses from *The Mistress*. Swift changes the title to *Clad all in Brown* (iii, 146), and proceeds to cover with filth his detested and despised enemy Richard Tighe. This is again a poem which can be regarded either as the product of a diseased imagination or as a contemptuous revolt against poetic sentiment. Here are a few lines of the original and the parody:

Fairest thing that shines below, . . .	Foulest brute that stinks below, . . .
So clouds themselves like Suns appear, When the Sun pierces them with Light: . . .	Not one jot better looks the sun Seen from behind a dirty clout. . . .
So Lillies in a glass enclose,	So t—ds within a glass enclose,

The Glass will seem as white as those. . . .	The glass will seem as brown as those. . . .
Such robes the Saints departed wear, Woven all with Light divine. . . .	Old carted bawds such garments wear, When pelted all with dirt they shine; . . .

It is little to be wondered at that some of his contemporaries declared that there was no traditional name for such a writer as this. In *Gulliveriana*, 1728, Dean Smedley describes Swift's verse as follows:

"Low, groveling Poetry all of it; and I challenge all the World, to show one good *Epic*, *Elegiac* or *Lyric* Poem of his; one *Eclogue*, *Pastoral*, or anything like the Antients; and as he can't write like them, so they had no name for such a Writer as he is: And his *Doggerel* and *Burlesque* had Banish'd him *Rome*, notwithstanding he is so often huzza'd in *Dublin*."

In 1733 Swift wrote an admirable reply to this criticism of his practice of poetry; it is a long piece, entitled *To a Lady, who desired the author to write some verses upon her in the heroic style* (ii, 26.). She asks him to

> suspend a while
> That same paltry, burlesque style;
> Drop for once your constant rule,
> Turning all to ridicule;

She will provide him with material, and he is to try instead to sing her praise in strain sublime. But the attempt is vain; he allows her due praise, but instinctively turns to give her advice, and then offers this apology:

> To conclude this long essay;
> Pardon if I disobey,
> Nor against my natural vein,
> Treat you in heroic strain.
> I, as all the parish knows,
> Hardly can be grave in prose:
> Still to lash, and lashing smile,
> Ill befits a lofty style.
> From the planet of my birth
> I encounter vice with mirth.

Then he turns to have a fling at kings and courts, and corrupt ministers, but here too constantly insists that his only method of treating all such things is ridicule.

> Safe within my little wherry,
> All their madness makes me merry:
> Like the waterman of Thames,
> I row by, and call them names;
> Like the ever-laughing sage,
> In a jest I spend my rage:
> (Though it must be understood,
> I would hang them if I could;)

And he concludes:

> For your sake as well as mine,
> I the lofty style decline.
> I should make a figure scurvy,
> And your head turn topsy-turvy.

When Faulkner published the volume of collected poems, it was prefaced by an *Advertisement*, dated Dublin 1734, which must have been approved if not written by Swift.

The collection is said to consist chiefly "of Humour or Satyr, and very often of both together". And the one claim that is made for the Poems is that at any rate they do not follow the old well-trodden paths: "the Author never was known either in Verse or Prose to borrow any Thought, Simile, Epithet, or particular Manner of Style: but whatever he writ, whether good, bad, or indifferent, is an Original in itself."

Twenty years later, it was pointed out in the *Connoisseur* (No. 67) that a great age in literature is always marked by variety and originality, and its authors are distinguished by cultivating different branches of poetry from each other. "We admire Swift, Pope, Gay, Bolingbroke, Addison, etc., but we admire each for his particular beauties separate and distinguished from the rest." At least during the eighteenth century it was not forgotten that the poetry of the Augustans was both original and varied; the differences were never merged together under some stupid generalization, merely for the convenience of the historian in contrasting them with something else. Even Dr. Elrington Ball is inclined I think to give too much importance to Swift's association with Addison and Prior, though strangely enough he makes no reference whatever to Samuel Butler. If we wish to account for the particular quality of Swift's verse, if we wish to place him in a tradition, we shall have to investigate first of all what he owed to *Hudibras*, and to the popular verse-satire of the seventeenth century.

Swift was, however, like his contemporaries in claiming that all his satire, whether concerning public affairs or the manners of society, "hath no other Aim than to reform the Errors of both Sexes". Many of his critics, as well in the eighteenth century as in the twentieth, have not been satisfied with this explanation of such poems as *The Lady's Dressing Room*, *A beautiful young Nymph going to Bed*, and *Strephon and Chloe*. I will pass over the usual objections, and consider only a very recent attack from an unexpected quarter; for it is particularly interesting to find that Mr. Aldous Huxley and D. H. Lawrence were distressed by these poems.

The latter objects in an essay entitled *Apropos of Lady Chatterley's Lover* (1930), that Swift in *The Lady's Dressing Room* (which he refers to in a very misleading fashion as a poem "to his mistress Celia") gives evidence of a mind diseased by "terror of the body".

"A great wit like Swift could not see how ridiculous he made himself. . . . Think of poor Celia, made to feel iniquitous about her proper natural function, by her lover. It is monstrous. And it comes from having taboo words, and from not keeping the mind sufficiently developed in physical and sexual consciousness."

And yet of course Swift had no taboo words, and shocked even some of his eighteenth century readers because he manifests that so clearly in this very poem, and because he was willing to bring so much at any rate of the physical into consciousness. The whole significance of these poems lies in the fact that Swift hated the sentimentality of the ordinary romantic love-stuff. He is repeating here— even more drastically—what he had done in the poems already referred to, *The Progress of Beauty*, and *Clad all in Brown*. Instead of rapturously describing the beauty of the body, or the poetry of dress, and all that stimulates desire, he is as usual turning things upside down, and with

complete lack of restraint exposing the ugliness and un-
pleasantness of certain physical functions, and of certain
aspects of private life in English fashionable society of the
time, which were usually kept hidden. What squeamish
people really object to is that in such poems Swift, as
he readily admits, mingles humour with satire. They
cannot forgive him because, in the very act of uncovering
these unsavoury things, instead of making a horrified
grimace, he is able to grin: it is in accordance with his
experience—

> Thus, I find it by experiment,
> Scolding moves you less than merriment.
> I may storm and rage in vain;
> It but stupefies your brain.
> But with raillery to nettle,
> Sets your thoughts upon their mettle.

Mr. Aldous Huxley's essay on *Swift* (included in *What You
Will*, 1929) is a brilliant elaboration of the same point. It
is suspicious, however, in the first place because of the
violence of his language. He quotes a casual remark of
Swift's from a letter to Stella "(I hate the word bowels)"
and then continues excitedly:

"Yes, how he hated it! And not the word only—the
things too, the harmless necessary tripes—he loathed and
detested them with an intensity of hatred such as few men
have ever been capable of. It was unbearable to him that
men should go through life with guts and sweetbreads,
with liver and lights, spleens and kidneys." . . . All this
was "a source of excruciating suffering" . . . "his resentment
was incredibly bitter."

Did it ever occur to Mr. Huxley in the first place that the word "bowels" had been used (in its metaphorical and sentimental sense) throughout the seventeenth century by all the canting preachers whom Swift most detested, till the very sound of it must have been unendurable in his ears. Even the few references given in the *New English Dictionary* are significant enough. There is a Parliamentary Proclamation for 1651, which refers to "Want of bowels in preaching towards them who are in hazard to perish". Fuller could not resist quoting a horrible pun in 1655: "Bloody Bonner . . . full (as one said) of guts, and empty of bowels." And this continued into the eighteenth century, as for instance in this delightful phrase from the *London Gazette* just a little earlier than Swift's protest: "To shew their bowels for their country".

I doubt very much Mr. Huxley's remark that Swift loathed "the things too, the harmless necessary tripes". It seems to me only a proof of the extreme sensitiveness of the twentieth century humorist that accounts for his abhorrent disgust at Swift's unsavoury jokes. And, I am sure, a little further acquaintance with Swift would prevent Mr. Huxley from writing such a sentence as this: "Swift's greatness lies in the intensity, the almost insane violence of that "hatred of bowels" which is the essence of his misanthropy and which underlies the whole of his work." Is this not to forget a little too obviously that the Dean of St. Patrick's was in the first place a wit and a humorist?

But, to return to the poems, is it fantastic to suggest that *Strephon and Chloe* can be most fairly judged, if it is regarded as a burlesque Epithalamium? At least it is a satire on a subject which always drove Swift to violent ridicule—romantic nonsense about marriage, a poison which he always feared as a great menace to human happiness. Whenever he speaks of marriage it is with almost incredible detachment and cold reasonableness. In one of his earliest letters it will be remembered that he had written to Varina to make a proposal of marriage. After a long list of questions, which he had always resolved to put to her with whom he meant to pass his life, he concludes: "whenever you can heartily answer them in the affirmative, I shall be blessed to have you in my arms, without regarding whether your person be beautiful, or your fortune large. Cleanliness in the first, and competency in the other is all I look for" (*Corr.* i, 35.) Again when asked for advice about getting married by his friend Knightley Chetwode, Swift replied. (Feb. 12, 1729-30.)

"As to changing your single life, it is impossible to advise without knowing all circumstances both of you and the. person. Archbishop Sheldon advised a young Lord to be sure to get money with a wife, because he would then be at least possessed of one good thing". (*Corr.* iv, 123.)

At any rate Swift always felt that it was a dangerous business, and he endeavours repeatedly in his poem *Strephon and Chloe* (ii, 4) to make his moral purpose clear. He allows full play to his satirical wit in picturing Strephon's fall out of the clouds of romance, but constantly interrupts his story to give advice of the plainest kind:

> Since husbands get behind the scene,
> The wife should study to be clean;
>
> .   .   .   .
>
> Authorities, both old and recent,
> Direct that women must be decent;

> And from the spouse each blemish hide,
> More than from all the world beside.

And the concluding moral is almost too commonplace and
serious:

> On sense and wit your passion found,
> By decency cemented round;
> Let prudence with good-nature strive,
> To keep esteem and love alive.
> Then come old age whene'er it will,
> Your friendship shall continue still;
> And thus a mutual gentle fire
> Shall never but with life expire.

We are reminded of a splendid tribute to Swift, in one of
Arbuthnot's letters, written on September 20, 1726:

"I had a great deal of discourse with your friend, her
Royal Highness. She insisted upon your wit, and good
conversation. I told her Royal Highness, that was not
what I valued you for, but for being a sincere honest man,
and speaking truth when others were afraid to speak it".
(*Corr.* iii, 343.)

But it was that indeed which was the very source of Swift's
wit; he needed only to say with his perfect simplicity and
directness what he saw to be true, and to most of his
readers who live perpetually in a world of romance and
sentiment, it seemed the most biting irony. To them he
appeared a mad fellow indeed, turning everything to wit
and foolery—friendship and hate, love and marriage, and
at last, death and judgment.

Even Lucretius, in his argument against the fear of

death, allows that death brings grief for those who are left behind:

> But we, thy friends, shall all those sorrows find,
> Which in forgetful death thou leav'st behind;
> No time shall dry our tears, nor drive them from our mind.
> (Dryden's translation of the latter part of
> the Third Book, included in *Sylvae*, 1685.)

But Swift turns even this to scorn, with his motto from La Rochefoucauld, which he takes as his theme for the *Verses on the Death of Dr. Swift*, published in 1739: (ii, 81.)

> "In all distresses of our friends,
> We first consult our private ends;
> While nature, kindly bent to ease us,
> Points out some circumstance to please us."

The poem is an "apologia pro vita sua", and characteristically concerned more with what he was and did, than with what he wrote. He does, however, repeat once more his favourite boast that "what he writ was all his own" and

> . . . with a moral view design'd
> To cure the vices of mankind:

but finally admits:

> "Perhaps I may allow the Dean
> Had too much satire in his vein;
> And seem'd determin'd not to starve it,
> Because no age could more deserve it."

But that does not restrain him from one last stroke—beautifully expressive of the way in which so often he mingled generosity and contempt.

> "He gave the little wealth he had
> To build a house for fools and mad;
> And show'd by one satiric touch,
> No nation wanted it so much."

There is not much further scope left for wit and satire. But after his death there was found among his papers, in his own handwriting, a poem on *The Day of Judgment* (ii, 17.) It was very fitting that it was first printed as quoted by Lord Chesterfield, in a letter to Voltaire, dated August 27, 1752.

It describes the Last Day, with the world standing trembling before Jove's throne, and then gives very shortly the epilogue to the whole comedy of life:

> "Offending race of human kind,
> By nature, reason, learning, blind;
> You who, through frailty, stepp'd aside;
> And you, who never fell from pride:
> You who in different sects were shamm'd,
> And come to see each other damn'd;
> (So some folk told you, but they knew
> No more of Jove's designs than you;)
> —The world's mad business now is o'er,
> And I resent these pranks no more,
> —I to such blockheads set my wit!
> I damn such fools!—Go, go, you're bit."

Here is the complete triumph of the Comic Spirit, un-abashed and unafraid, delighting to overthrow all mankind's claims to dignity and importance, and "ending with a puff" the whole heroic and romantic delusion.

COLLINS AND THE CREATIVE IMAGINATION:
A STUDY IN THE CRITICAL BACKGROUND
OF HIS ODES (1746)[1]

A. S. P. Woodhouse

IF it be true that historical Romanticism means above all else the liberation of the imagination and the emotions, the views entertained of the imagination by poets and critics in the eighteenth century become data of the first importance to the historian of the Romantic movement. This fact has, of course, been fully recognized, for example by Professor Babbitt, through whom the writer's interest in the subject was first aroused, and by Mr. Logan Pearsall Smith, in his brilliant treatment of *Four Romantic Words*. Mr. Smith very properly fastens upon the emerging conception of *creative imagination* as the matter of primary significance, and he does not fail to recognize the important position held by the Wartons in the early evolution of this idea. The purpose of the present

---

[1] I must mention, with acknowledgment of aid received: M. W. Bundy's *Theory of the Imagination, Classical and Mediaeval* (*Univ. of Illinois Studies in Lang. and Lit.*, XII, ii-iii); his *"Invention" and "Imagination" in the Renaissance* (*Jour. of Eng. and Germ. Philol.*, XXIX, pp. 535 ff.); his *Bacon's True Opinion of Poetry* (*Studies in Philol.*, XXVII, pp. 244 ff.); L. P. Smith's *Four Romantic Words* (*Words and Idioms*, Boston, 1925); J. G. Robertson's *The Genesis of Romantic Theory*, Cambridge, 1923; Irving Babbitt's *Rousseau and Romanticism*, Boston, 1919; A. D. McKillop's *Romanticism of William Collins* (*Studies in Philol.*, XX, pp. 1 ff.); writings of R. D. Havens, cited below; and W. C. Bronson's excellent *Poems of William Collins*, Boston (1898), the edition from which I quote. In the case of other texts quoted, I have uniformly modernized spelling and punctuation. All italics are mine.

essay is, (i) to show, what has been heretofore unobserved, that William Collins has his interesting word to add to the Wartons' theory, as well as a potent illustration of that theory in his practice; (ii) to sketch rapidly the history of the imagination in English criticism, in order to place the views of Collins and Joseph Warton in their due historical perspective and to emphasize certain very necessary distinctions which could find little or no place in Mr. Smith's semantic study; (iii) to indicate some of the ways in which the views entertained of the imagination throw light on Collins's *Odes* (1746), and (iv) on their place in the history of eighteenth-century poetry and of developing Romanticism.

I

The *Ode on the Poetical Character* has always passed for Collins's most obscure poem. The eighteenth-century critic who found it as difficult as the forty-seventh proposition of Euclid has not been·alone in his opinion. Its full meaning has, I believe, never been expounded, though Mrs. Barbauld, curiously enough, was not far from the right track, and Coleridge's enthusiasm for the ode no doubt rested on a complete comprehension. The poem, in fact, appears to be an allegory in a somewhat stricter sense than Collins's remaining odes, an allegory whose subject is the *creative imagination* and the poet's passionate desire for its power.

The magic girdle, described in the strophe, evidently symbolizes the endowment of the true poet. Two facts immediately equate this endowment with the possession of imagination in a superlative degree: it is in Fancy's gift; and it enables its possessor 'to gaze her visions wild':

> Young Fancy thus, to me divinest name,
>   To whom, prepar'd and bath'd in heav'n,
>   The cest of amplest pow'r is giv'n,
>   To few the godlike gift assigns,
>   To gird their blest prophetic loins,
> And gaze her visions wild, and feel unmix'd her
>   flame.

Unlike the school of Taste, the followers of Shaftesbury, Collins regards the poet not as a being of exquisitely balanced faculties,[1] but one endowed "to some divine excess" with this single power, or perhaps with imagination accompanied by an unusual capacity for feeling.[2] Fancy can vouchsafe 'visions'; and these evidently transcend ordinary experience and are productive of wonder, not untouched by terror. The poet would see,

> appall'd, th' unreal scene
> While Fancy lifts the veil between.[3]

The epode[4] Bronson is content to summarize as "the weaving of the magic girdle of poetry" and to pronounce

[1] "For taste does not wholly depend upon the natural strength and acquired improvement of the intellectual powers, nor wholly upon a fine construction of the organs of the body, nor wholly upon the intermediate powers of the imagination, but upon a union of them all happily blended, without too great prevalency in either (*sic*)" (John Gilbert Cooper, *Letters concerning Taste*, 3rd edit., London, 1757, p. 27). Cooper also speaks, however, of "that unconstrained fire of imagination which constitutes the true poet" (*ibid.*, p. 28).

[2] *Cf. Ode to Fear*, l. 69.

[3] *Ibid.*, ll. 2-4.

[4] Thus named by Bronson, following Collins's practice elsewhere. Actually, of course, it is a mesode.

"the most obscure passage in Collins."[5] Mrs. Barbauld
defines Collins's underlying idea thus, "that true poetry,
being a representation of nature, must have its archetype
in those ideas of the Supreme Mind which originally gave
birth to nature."[6] This is not quite the relation which
Collins proposes, for to him poetry is not primarily concerned with nature, but with a bright world of ideal forms.
What he would suggest is that the activity of the poetic
imagination is creative, that it makes its own world; and
to this end he describes God's act of creation as itself a
flight of the Divine Imagination: God

> call'd with thought to birth
> Yon tented sky, this laughing earth.

What follows is, as Bronson happily says, distinctly "suggestive of Jupiter Amans";[7] but the meaning seems perfectly clear. The "lov'd enthusiast" is Fancy, and it is
she who co-operates in the act of creation. In other words,
we have an allegorical repetition of the fact already simply
stated: God imagined the world, and it sprang into being:

> Long by the lov'd enthusiast woo'd,
> Himself in some diviner mood,

[5]The obscurity is due to the fact that Collins injects an account of
the creation between ll. 23-4, where he suggests that he is about to
describe the weaving of the girdle, and ll. 41-50, where he fulfils the
promise; perhaps also to some suddenness of transition at l. 41, which,
however, is common in Collins and was, further, regarded as a feature of
the Pindaric ode.

[6]William Collins, *Poet. Works*, with prefatory essay by Mrs. Barbauld, 2nd edit., London, 1802, p. xxiv.

[7]Mrs. Barbauld had been deeply shocked: Collins's "allegory is
neither luminous nor decent"!

Retiring, sate with her alone,
And plac'd her on his sapphire throne,
The whiles, the vaulted shrine around,
Seraphic wires were heard to sound,
Now sublimest triumph swelling,
Now on love and mercy dwelling;
And she, from out the veiling cloud,
Breath'd her magic notes aloud:
And thou, thou rich-hair'd Youth of Morn,
And all thy subject life, was born.[8]

It was at this time, as the poet has told us, that the magic cestus (symbol of the poet's endowment, *i.e.*, of the poetic imagination) was produced. The inference is, I think, inevitable, that the activity of the poetic imagination is, in some sort, a counterpart of the divine act of creation, that the poet, too, is a creator, as the critics of the Renaissance were fond of asserting, that Fancy and Heaven are, in Collins's own phrase, "kindred powers."

The poet now passes from his general account of the "creating day" to the particular description of the weaving

[8]The "rich-hair'd Youth of Morn" is, of course, the sun; his "subject life", the living things on earth, dependent on his rays. The sources of the imagery in the poem form an interesting study, but I do not wish to obscure the argument by discussing them here. It is, however, relevant to observe that the association of Fancy with the Deity may well have been suggested by the like allegorical association of Wisdom with God in *Proverbs* viii, 23-30. We happen to know that Joseph Warton greatly admired the passage as an instance of poetic personification. He paraphrases it in his discussion of the subject (*Adventurer*, No. 57). Is it not possible that Collins, writing an allegorical poem on the idea of the creative imagination, held in common by Warton and himself, should have remembered the magnificent personification which they had, perhaps, admired together?

of the girdle. As the "sainted growing woof" takes shape, other figures grace the scene, and these may be expected to have a special significance:

> near it sate ecstatic Wonder,
> List'ning the deep applauding thunder,
> And Truth in sunny vest array'd,

while

> All the shad'wy tribes of mind
> In braided dance their murmurs join'd,
> And all the bright uncounted Pow'rs
> Who feed on heav'n's ambrosial flow'rs.

These are not difficult of interpretation: Truth would symbolize the validity of the poet's imagining; Wonder emphasizes anew the effect for which Collins chiefly looks in poetry; "the shadowy tribes of mind" are the bright allegorical figures of which his odes are all compact; the "uncounted powers" are the angels of Milton (immediately to be adduced as an example of true poetic endowment), or, more generally, those spiritual beings which in Collins, as in Addison, appear in conjunction with "the shadowy tribes of mind."

The antistrophe introduces Milton as the outstanding instance of the creative imagination in English poetry and hails him as Collins's guide.[9] The poem then closes on a note of disillusion, already struck in the concluding lines of strophe and epode: it is, indeed, a sort of sombre burden, sounding with increasing emphasis through the ode. Collins has already paused in mid-career to ask:

[9]Collins's avowed discipleship of Milton is accompanied, as in the case of Joseph and Thomas Warton's discipleship of Shakespeare and Spenser (*Enthusiast*, ll. 170-81; *Pleasures of Melancholy*, ll. 151-6) by a

Where is the bard whose soul can now
Its high presuming hopes avow?
Where he who thinks, with rapture blind,
This hallow'd work for him design'd?

And now he declares his discipleship of Milton to have been

In vain—such bliss to one alone
Of all the sons of soul was known,
And Heav'n and Fancy, kindred pow'rs,
Have now o'erturn'd th' inspiring bow'rs,
Or curtain'd close such scene from ev'ry future view.

His disillusion with the poetic powers of his age anticipates Blake's in *To the Muses*, or Gray's when he exclaims, in his *Stanzas to Bentley*,

But not to one in this benighted age
Is that diviner inspiration giv'n,
That burns in Shakespeare's or in Milton's page,
The pomp and prodigality of heav'n!

The words of disillusion and self-distrust must be given their due weight, but so also must the account of the poetic endowment which precedes them.   The subject of the ode

repudiation of the Neo-classical school which has intervened between these distant models and their admirers; but Collins, instead of mentioning Pope or Addison, goes back to the first poet in whom neo-classical practice is at all fully illustrated, Milton's contemporary, Waller.   There is a further suggestion, absent in the Wartons, that the poet's own development can be, in part, summed up as a substitution of the influence of Milton for that of Waller and his school.

is *The Poetical Character*[10]; and the poet's despair can be understood only in so far as one has comprehended his ideal of that character, has grasped, that is, his belief in the primacy of the imagination and in its creative activity.

[10]I am aware that my interpretation of the poem runs counter to that of Mr. H. W. Garrod. I would not have my statement of the grounds of my disagreement suggest any lack of respect for this eminent scholar. He holds (*Collins*, Oxford, 1928, p. 59) that the poem "is, in effect, an ode on the poetical character of Milton", though Milton is not mentioned till l. 64, and then as an example, or if it is preferred, *the* example of the creative imagination. He insists (p. 69) that the "rich-hair'd Youth of Morn" (l. 39) is not the sun, but "the Poet, who has the rich or long hair of all poets and of Apollo, father of poets." This exegesis necessitates a desperate emendation of the text (l. 40), to read,

And all thy subject—Life—was born!

If the "rich-hair'd Youth of Morn" is the sun ("the bright-hair'd sun" of the *Ode to Evening*—that is to say, Apollo in his rôle of sun-god), the "subject life" means the vegetable and animal life on earth, which is dependent on (subject to) the sun. This is sense and current English in 1746 or 1931. If, however, the "rich-hair'd Youth of Morn" is the Poet, it is nonsense; hence the emendation. "Life", Mr. Garrod argues in effect, must be in apposition to "subject"; the poet's subject-matter is life. This, too, makes sense; but is it at all usual eighteenth-century phrasing? When an eighteenth-century critic wants to indicate that the poet draws his materials from what we call "life", he speaks of him as imitating *nature*. It is true that in *The Manners* (l. 22) Collins talks of "Life's wide prospect", but he means *human* life. Mr. Garrod is somewhat startled by Collins's (or his own) fiction of the Poet, "born" from the union of Fancy and the Deity. But "born" is clearly used figuratively for "created", exactly as is "birth" at an earlier point in the same passage (ll. 25-6): no one is born; the sun is created by the imagination of God. Mr. Garrod thinks (pp. 65-6) that in repudiating Waller's *myrtle shades* (l. 69) "Collins describes himself as withdrawing from love poetry" and that the direction of his new effort is hinted in the *Ode to Simplicity* (ll. 51-4), which the critic interprets as a promise to write pastorals. We are used to unfulfilled promises in Collins; but to

II

The conception of thé poet as a creator was, of course, common enough in Renaissance criticism. A typical passage is the well-known one from Sidney:

"Neither let it be deemed too saucy a comparison to

learn that he repudiates love-poetry (which he had not written) in favour of pastorals (which he was not to write) is a little bewildering. The "pastorals" lie outside my present field (though it would be easy to show that the cited passage by no means necessarily implied any such promise). As to the repudiation of Waller, all turns on the epithet *myrtle* and the original association of the myrtle with Venus. Does that association persist wherever in English poetry the *myrtle* is mentioned as part of the poet's garland, for example, in *Lycidas*, l. 2? And what of Collins's use of the word elsewhere? In the *Epistle to Hanmer* (ll. 2-4) the Muse

sees her *myrtles* bloom,
Green and unwither'd o'er his (Shakespeare's) honour'd tomb;

but does Collins associate the poetic treatment of love with Shakespeare? On the contrary, he holds, with Joseph Warton, that preoccupation with this passion is a mark of decadence in poetry and that Shakespeare manifests his strength by dealing largely with other passions. Elaborating comments on Fletcher and Shakespeare, found in Dryden (*Essay of Dramatic Poesy* and *On the Grounds of Criticism in Tragedy*), Collins declares (*Epistle to Hanmer*, ll. 61-6) that Fletcher presents

Each melting sigh, and ev'ry tender tear,
The lover's wishes, and the virgin's fear. . . .
But stronger Shakespeare felt for man alone:
Drawn by his pen, our ruder passions stand
Th' unrivall'd picture of his early hand.

(The passages to which I have referred generally above, are: *Epistle to Hanmer*, ll. 39-42, 57-66; *Ode to Simplicity*, ll. 37-9; Joseph Warton's *Essay on Pope*, London, 1806, I, pp. 258-61, and his paper on *Lear*, *Adventurer*, No. 113).

balance the highest point of man's wit with the efficacy of
nature: but rather give right honour to the heavenly
Maker of the maker, who, having made man to His own
likeness, set him beyond and over all the works of that second nature; which in nothing he sheweth so much as *in
poetry, when with the force of a divine breath, he bringeth things
forth far surpassing her doings. . . .*[1]"

Or take as a later example these forceful lines, addressed
by Cowley to the Muse:

> Whatever God did say
> Is all thy plain and smooth, uninterrupted way.
> Nay, ev'n beyond His works thy voyages are known:
> Thou hast thousand worlds too of thine own;
> Thou speak'st, great Queen! in the same style as He,
> And a new world leaps forth when thou say'st, Let it be![2]

In neither of the instances selected does one find the poet's
creativeness completely equated with the activity of the
imagination. Sidney indeed seeks to combine an emphasis
on *invention*, already associated with imagination,[3] and
later to assume renewed importance in Pope's *Preface to
Homer*, and an emphasis on imitation, which, in its Aristotelian form,[4] is, as Sidney saw, perfectly compatible with

[1]*Apology for Poetry, Elizabethan Critical Essays*, ed. G. Gregory
Smith, Oxford, 1904, I, p. 157.

[2]Anderson's *British Poets*, V, pp. 301-2.

[3]See M. W. Bundy's article on *"Invention"* and *"Imagination"*,
cited above.

[4]In its Platonic form the doctrine of imitation is inimical to the idea
of creation, despite Plato's own remark: ". . . Imitation is a kind of
creation—of images, however, not of real things" (*Sophist*, trans.
Jowett).

the idea of creation. Cowley is content to introduce into his allegory, as the steeds of the Muse's chariot, the related conceptions of Wit, Fancy, and Invention. A clearer equation of creativeness with imaginative activity is found in Puttenham's *Art of English Poesy*:

"A poet is . . . . a maker . . . . Such as, by way of resemblance and reverently, we may say of God, who without any travail to His divine imagination made all the world of nought, nor also by any pattern or mould, as the Platonics, with their ideas, do fantastically suppose: even so the very poet makes and contrives out of his own brain both the verse and matter of his poem, and not by any foreign copy or example. . . . ."[5]

While seeking, like Sidney, to bring his theory into harmony with the Aristotelian idea of imitation, Puttenham is inclined to explain poetic creation by reference to the rival Platonic doctrine of inspiration, to 'some divine instinct— the Platonics call it *furor*.'[6]

In Milton, too, the theory of inspiration can, by dint of analysis, be brought into some connection with the imagination, though at first glance one might well suppose that Collins, finding his chief example of creative imagination in Milton, would look in vain for confirmatory theory in the poet. In the fifth book of *Paradise Lost* Milton, through Adam, declares his belief in the supremacy of

[5]*Elizabethan Critical Essays*, II, p. 3; *cf. ibid.*, II, pp. 19-20, where Puttenham develops his ideas of the poetic imagination. Puttenham's work was a favourite with Collins's friend Thomas Warton, who cites it some fifteen times in his *Observations on the Faery Queen* and *History of English Poetry*.

[6]*Elizabethan Critical Essays*, II, p. 3.

reason, and while making clear the legitimate subordinate function of the imagination, voices his distrust of that faculty.[7]   For when reason is in abeyance, as for example in sleep, the inferior image-forming faculty usurps her place:

> Oft in her absence mimic Fancy wakes
> To imitate her; but, misjoining shapes,
> Wild work produces oft. . . . .

But how, if, in the abeyance of reason, imagination should not be left to play the mimic uncontrolled?   How if some power, superior even to reason, should intervene and join the shapes—direct the imagination, in short?   Milton does not ask these questions,—but he answers them.   It is in the abeyance of reason that inspiration comes:

> . . . . my celestial patroness who deigns
> Her nightly visitation unimplored,
> And dictates to me slumbering, or inspires
> Easy my unpremeditated verse. . . .[8]

But is it the imagination that is thus inspired?   Again, by implication, Milton answers in Adam's words:

> Mine eyes he closed, *but open left the cell*
> *Of fancy, my internal sight.*[9]

[7]Ll. 100-13.   It is to be noted that Milton (V, ll. 486-7) distinguishes between two modes of reason, the discursive and the immediate or intuitive.   The time was to come when romantic theory would describe the second mode as imagination, and imagination as "reason in her most exalted mood" (Wordsworth, *Prelude*, XIV, ll. 189-92).

[8]*Par. Lost*, IX, ll. 21-4.

[9]*Ibid.*, VIII, ll. 460-1.

Such dark and interlinear sayings can, however, have had little influence.

Very different is the case of Bacon, whose general theory of the imagination is somewhat similar to that later adopted by Milton, but whose attitude towards poetry is quite dissimilar. Discarding alike the theories of imitation and of inspiration current in his day, Bacon concentrates on the poet's creativeness, which he attributes wholly to the activity of the imagination.[10] But to pause here is to tell only half the story. Bacon may emphasize the place of imagination in poetry, but at bottom he distrusts both the faculty and its products. Imagination "being not tied to the laws of matter, may at pleasure join that which nature hath severed, and sever that which nature hath joined, and make unlawful matches and divorces of things." If he wrote about science like a lord chancellor, he certainly wrote about poetry like a scientist. For him the creations of the poetic imagination have a certain use, but no final validity. Indeed it might be said, with only a pardonable degree of exaggeration, that for Bacon the poet's creativeness and his usefulness alike are purchased at the expense of truth: "The use of this feigned history hath been to give some shadow of satisfaction to the mind of man in those points wherein the nature of things doth deny it. . . ." Poetry "was ever thought to have some participation of divineness because it doth raise and erect the mind by submitting the shows of things to the desires of the mind; whereas reason doth buckle and bow the mind to the nature of things." Bacon plainly would not have con-

[10] *Advancement of Learning*, II; *De Augmentis*, V, i; *Descriptio Globi Intellectualis*, i; *Philos. Works*, ed. J. M. Robertson, London, 1905, pp. 87-9, 499-500, 677-8.

ceded that Truth was by when the magic girdle of Fancy was weaving; nor would he have mistaken imagination for 'reason in her most exalted mood'. For him the two faculties are in sharp antithesis: reason *works* and discovers truth; imagination *plays* and affords diversion.[11] And the inevitable result is that contempt which attends poetry when it is separated from reality and regarded as a mere diversion or a mere narcotic: "As for poesy, it is rather a pleasure or play of imagination than a work or duty thereof;" and again, "But it is not good to stay too long in the theatre. Let us now pass on to the judicial place or palace of the mind, which we are to approach and view with more reverence and attention."

In his picture of poetry shaping a world nearer to the heart's desire, Bacon stands at the head of a long romantic tradition;[12] in his sharp antithesis between imagination and reason he occupies ground common to the Neo-classicists and the majority of Romantics; in his assignment of poetry to the imagination he was ultimately to become an important critical force making for Romanticism,[13] but in his depreciation of poetry as the mere play of imagination, there can be little doubt that he exercised for a time a directly contrary influence. His inherited prejudice against

[11]Bacon's enthusiasm for "parabolical" poetry may be traced (as Mr. Bundy has suggested) to his sense that here imagination is operating under the control of reason and to her ends.

[12]The statement refers to Bacon's influence, not to his own originality, which, Mr. Bundy finds, has been exaggerated.

[13]For a cautious estimate see J. G. Robertson, *Genesis of Romantic Theory*, pp. 235 ff.

the imagination was shared by the Neo-classical critics.[14] His accentuation of this prejudice must have had its effect, especially among the growing body of his disciples. Dissatisfied with a relegation of poetry to the field of pleasant falsehoods, the critics sought to ground the art not on the *play* of fancy, but on the *work* of reason, on what they variously described as 'reason', as 'judgment', or merely as 'good sense':

"And whereas poems which are produced by the vigour of imagination only have a gloss upon them at the first, which time wears off, the works of judgment are like the diamond; the more they are polished, the more lustre they receive."[15]

To imagination they assigned the subordinate function of adornment: "Judgment begets the strength and structure, and Fancy begets the ornaments of a poem;"[16]

> Fancy is but the feather on the pen;
> Reason is that substantial, useful part
> Which gains the head, while t'other wins the heart.[17]

---

[14]Instances abound during the hundred years which separates Hobbes's statement, "Without steadiness and direction to some end a great fancy is one kind of madness" (*Leviathan*, 1651), and Johnson's, "All power of fancy over reason is a degree of insanity" (*Rasselas*, 1759), but more especially before Addison's *Spectator* papers.

[15]Dryden, *Dedication of the Aeneis, Essays*, ed. W. P. Ker, Oxford, 1900, II, p. 225.

[16]Hobbes, *Answer to Davenant, Critical Essays of the Seventeenth Century*, ed. J. E. Spingarn, Oxford, 1908, II, p. 59.

[17]Sheffield, *Essay upon Poetry, ibid.*, II, p. 287.

Even in lyric poetry, says Edward Young, judgment, "that masculine power of the mind . . . . should bear the supreme sway, and a beautiful imagination, as a mistress, should be subdued to its dominion."[18] Imagining became mere 'imaging.'[19] Wit, which at times connoted the free activity of the imagination,[20]came increasingly to suggest 'imaging' duly subordinated to judgment, and finally even judgment itself:

"And in any discourse whatsoever, if the defect of discretion be apparent, how extravagant soever the fancy be, the whole discourse will be taken for a sign of want of wit.

". . . . Judgment, therefore, without fancy is wit, but fancy without judgment, not."[21]

> Some to whom Heav'n in wit has been profuse
> Want as much more to turn it to its use—[22]

where the wanted wit clearly connotes judgment. In Dryden's prefaces imagination for the most part assumes its attenuated meaning of 'imaging', and wit from being

[18]*On Lyric Poetry* (1728), *Poet. Works*, ed. J. Mitford, Boston, 1854' II, p. 161.

[19]The word is indeed used by Dryden ("*Imaging* is in itself the very height and life of poetry"—*Apology for Heroic Poetry*). This restriction of imagination to the parts of a poem, the individual images, as distinct from the whole, was fostered by Hobbes's close association of imagination with memory (*cf. Leviathan*, chap. iii).

[20]"Wit . . . is no other than the faculty of imagination in the poet" (Dryden, Preface to *Annus Mirabilis*). *Cf.* Bacon, *Of Studies*: "Histories make men wise; poets *witty*; the mathematics subtle . . ."— perhaps the earliest example of the connotation in question.

[21]Hobbes, *Leviathan*, London, 1885, p. 40.

[22]Pope, *Essay on Criticism*, ll. 80-1. See Churton Collins's discussion of Pope's use of the word.

equated with imagination (in this sense but with some added reference to invention) sinks to a mere "propriety in thoughts and words,"[23] the result of fancy operating in strict subordination to judgment.

To pursue further this concerted effort at grounding the art of poetry upon reason is immediately to encounter the Neo-classical reference of art to nature,

"At once the source, and end, and test of art."

In thinking of poetry as, in traditional terms, an *imitation of nature*, the Neo-classicist inevitably set a limit to its range, the limit of his own conception of *nature*. That term had, of course, a variety of connotations; but what may be called its basic meaning seems to have been *the sum total of truth as experience and reason, working in union, ascertained it*; so that poetry was limited to the depiction of a world that was rational, ordered, unmysterious, and rather commonplace, though it is clearly possible for the imagination to figure forth a world that is none of these things. Accordingly, the reference of art to nature, as nature was commonly understood, must be reckoned among the forces which exercised a depressing influence on the rôle assigned to the imagination by Neo-classical criticism. We shall find that when Addison comes to deal with imagination in its more creative moments, the reference temporarily breaks down ("the poet quite loses sight of nature"), and this despite Addison's persistent association of the imagination with memory. We shall further find that the relation of the poet's imagining to nature, variously conceived, is the subject of somewhat conflicting pronounce-

[23]Contrast Preface to *Annus Mirabilis* with *Apology for Heroic Poetry*, Preface to *Sylvae*, Preface to *Albion and Albanius* (*Essays*, ed. Ker, I, pp. 14-15, 190, 256, 270).

ments by the eighteenth-century critics; none of them faces the question with boldness save Blake, but the utterances of Thomson, Akenside, and Joseph Warton, to be quoted later, will scarcely be fully understood unless the long-established reference of art to nature is kept in mind. Meanwhile, another aspect of this matter must not be wholly neglected. The reader who remembers such documents as Dryden's *Parallel of Poetry and Painting*, will very properly object that the *imitation of nature*, as sponsored by the Neo-classical critics, did not necessarily preclude the disciplined activity of the imagination, that the elements of idealization and creation inherent in Aristotle's use of the term were not completely forgotten. This is undoubtedly true. The word *nature*, as Professor Lovejoy remind us,[24] had at least two meanings which were differentiated somewhat sharply from its meaning of *empirical reality*: it meant *a collection of generic types*; or again it meant *a collection of the essences or Platonic ideas of kinds* (sometimes rendered more specific by the phrase *la belle nature*). And the *imitation of nature* in either of these senses, but especially in the latter (the sense found in Dryden's *Parallel*), certainly carries us, as it carried Dryden, to the idea of *invention as one of the qualities of the poet*. Nevertheless, I think that one detects in Neo-classical criticism a very marked tendency to accept the reference of art to nature without stopping to define the second term, and consequently a very marked tendency on the part of the term itself to slip from these critical heights into its commonplace meaning of *empirical reality* or, with the slightly more philosophical critic, into the meaning

[24]*Nature as an Aesthetic Norm* (*M. L. N.*, XLII, pp. 444 ff.).

suggested above, *truth as experience and reason have ascertained it.*

In the Neo-classical treatment of the imagination, then, several distinct steps deserve attention. There is the inherited distrust of the faculty and the effort to gain validity for poetry by grounding it not on imagination, but on reason. There is the reduction of imagination to mere 'imaging' and its function to the adornment of actual fact or of reason's concepts, in strict subordination to judgment. It will be observed later that these reductions do in measure correspond to the place of imagination in the major writings of Dryden and Pope. There was indeed—and this is the final step to note—an inevitable tendency for the depressed and attenuated term 'imagination' to drop out of literary terminology. It seemed possible to formulate the rules of good writing, as these were understood, with but little reference to the faculty. Pope gets through his *Essay on Criticism* with one unimportant use of the word and with some three or four uses of ' wit' in the sense of imagination.[25] The result was that Addison, whatever the value of his essays on the imagination, had an important service to perform for English criticism in his rehabilitation of the term.

To *The Spectator*[26] may certainly be traced that revival

[25]Ll. 58, 590, 717, 80, 292. L. 590 admits that without imagination (wit) poets are dull. Ll. 80 and 292 are derogatory. The fact that Aristotle, and Pope's chief models, Horace and Boileau, formulate their rules without assigning any dominant rôle to the imagination as such, of course, explains in part the unimportant place which the term holds in Pope's *Essay.*

[26]Nos. 411-21: *On the Pleasures of the Imagination.* See, on these papers, W. J. Courthope's *History of English Poetry*, V, chap. iv, and J. G. Robertson's *Genesis of Romantic Theory*, pp. 235-49. E. K.

Broadus's *Addison as a Literary Critic* (Harvard dissertation, unprinted) contains a valuable rebuttal of B. Worsfold's extravagant claims for Addison, in his *Principles of Literary Criticism*, chap. v.

It is impossible in this paper to carry the discussion beyond the English field. One must observe, however, that the imagination had figured in Renaissance criticism in both Italy and France (see M. W. Bundy's *"Invention" and "Imagination"*, cited above), and that early in the eighteenth century Italian critics, partly, at least, in response to the influence of Bacon, had revived the question of its fundamental place in poetry. J. G. Robertson (*Genesis of Romantic Theory*, p. 242) hints that one of the sources of Addison's theories may have been Lodovico Antonio Muratori's *Della Perfetta Poesia italiana*, first published in 1706. The possibility of Collins's familiarity with this work, as well as with earlier Italian criticism, should certainly be kept in mind. Among much that is obviously irrelevant to our purpose, we find in Muratori's book certain ideas which harmonize with those presented in Collins's ode. Poetry is divine; it owes its inspiration to Heaven (*Della Perfetta Poesia*, I, i); its aim is to delight, and one great source of poetic pleasure is the marvellous (*cf.* Collins's emphasis on wonder as the effect to be aimed at in poetry); the marvellous, which is equated with the sublime, is achieved through the operation of the imagination (I, vii; *cf.* I, xi, xiv ff.). Muratori, unlike the early English romantic theorists, discusses the problem of the validity of poetry, the *truth* of the imagination's findings, and he couples with the imagination two other powers, intellect and judgment (I, vi-vii, ix-xi, xiv ff.). Collins, of course, does not enter upon this argument, but his placing of Truth alongside Wonder at the weaving of the magic girdle seems to suggest some consciousness of the problem. Muratori distinguishes three realms in which poetry may find its subject-matter; the first of these is the celestial (the realm of God, the angels, and the soul), though its more usual province is the human (I, vi). One recalls "the bright, uncounted powers" (angels), mentioned by Collins with "the shadowy tribes of mind" (personifications), as also present at the weaving of the girdle. But it is in his emphasis upon imagination as the great force in poetic creation (I, xiv ff.) that Muratori's importance and his chief influence are to be found. For a full summary and commentary, see J. G. Robertson, *op. cit.*, pp. 60-95.

of interest in the faculty of imagination from which the romantic theory of the creative imagination directly springs. The paper's importance is not to be measured by the novelty or the consistency of the views advanced. Fundamentally Addison's theory constitutes a very slight advance upon that of Hobbes and Dryden; but his attitude towards the imagination is distinctly more friendly and less reserved than that of the majority of Neo-classical critics. The "talent of affecting the imagination sets off all writing in general but is the very life and highest perfection of poetry. . . . ."[27] "A poet should take as much pains in forming his imagination as a philosopher in cultivating his understanding." But what does Addison mean by *imagination*?

". . . . (B)y the pleasures of imagination I mean only such pleasures as arise originally from sight . . . . I divide these pleasures into two kinds: . . . . those primary pleasures of the imagination which entirely proceed from such objects as are before our eyes, and . . . . those secondary pleasures of the imagination which flow from the ideas of visible objects when the objects are not actually before the eye but are called up into our memories or formed into agreeable visions of things that are either absent or fictitious."

Like Hobbes and Dryden[28], he associates the imagination

[27]The passages quoted are from *Spectator*, Nos. 421, 417, 411, 411, 419, 421, respectively.

[28]Throughout, Addison is influenced by these two writers, by Bacon, and by Locke. On imagination itself Locke had nothing new to say (*Human Understanding*, II, ii, 2, and II, xi, 2, 4, 6): the association with memory, the limitation of its findings by previous sense impressions, its power, nevertheless, to compound images, are all present in

with memory. He tends to equate its products with the recollection of visual impressions. At the same time, he emphasizes, from the first, the imagination's compounding power:

"We cannot, indeed, have a single image in the fancy that did not make its first entrance through the sight; but we have the power of retaining, altering, and compounding those images which we have once received, into all the varieties of picture and vision that are most agreeable to the imagination; for by this faculty a man in a dungeon is capable of entertaining himself with scenes and landscapes more beautiful than any that can be found in the whole compass of nature."

In his treatment of poetry Addison still discusses imagination mainly in relation to the parts of a poem (imagination is still 'imaging'), and indeed he deals almost exclusively with descriptive writing. Of "the shaping spirit of imagination" which can inform the whole, there is, in his papers, not one indubitable suggestion. Nevertheless, in speaking of the imagination's capacity, through its compounding power, to transcend nature in variety and beauty, and evolve beings without counterpart in the natural world,

Hobbes. Locke's doctrine of the ideality of secondary qualities, which made a great impression upon Addison, may have had its unconscious influence on Addison's view of the imagination by seeming to free that faculty in some small measure from immediate dependence upon the material world. Addison, like Joseph Warton after him, was a confirmed Longinian. His emphasis on the visual character of imagination receives some countenance from his favourite: Imagination is a faculty through which, "moved by enthusiasm and passion, you seem to see the things of which you speak and place them before the eyes of your hearers" (*On the Sublime*, xv, trans. A. O. Prickard).

he is led to remark that here is something like a creative activity. In "the fairy way of writing" the poet "quite loses sight of nature" and delights by carrying us "as it were into a new creation." Imagination "makes additions to nature and gives a greater variety to God's works." "It has something in it like creation: it bestows a kind of existence."

To Addison, then, equivocal as is his attitude, English literary theory owes the rehabilitating of *imagination* as an important critical term, the reassertion, if only incidentally, of the creative function of the poet, and the specific association of this creative function with the imagination. Moreover, there are in Addison's papers, as we shall have occasion to observe, some suggestions with a special bearing on Collins's odes: that descriptive writing is the special sphere of imagination, that the effect of strangeness is one which it can and may achieve, that fairies and other supernatural beings, as indeed superstitions in general, come within its range, that the "shadowy persons" of allegory are a proper subject for its exercise. Nor must it be supposed that what may be called the basic elements in Addison's theory, which certainly lingered in the mind of Joseph Warton, were without their influence on Collins: the poet conceives his art almost wholly in terms of visual imagery.

Some of the direct fruits of Addison's papers on the imagination are found in the utterances of Mallet, Thomson, Akenside, Collins, and the Wartons, and doubtless in those of many other writers, whose lineage is less easy to trace.[29]

[29]A new attitude towards the imagination is seen, for example, in the following: "Poetry depends much more on imagination than other arts, but is not on that account less reasonable than they; for

Whether the more liberal attitude towards the imagination found in Pope's *Preface to Homer*, as compared with that found in the *Essay on Criticism*, can be attributed to Addison's influence seems doubtful. Homer's genius resides mainly in his power of invention, which Pope constantly refers to his imagination or fancy. In the term 'invention' the idea of creativeness is implicit, and, unlike the term 'imagination,' it is hampered by no habitual association with the parts of the poem, the mere images. Pope finds evidence of 'the strength of this amazing invention' in the *Iliad* as a whole and in all its parts, from the fable, generally considered, through the characters and the individual scenes, down to the particular 'descriptions, images, and similes'. This fact, together with the specific re-association of invention with imagination, makes Pope's *Preface* a document of first-rate importance.[30]

Of the writers who are influenced by Addison, not only Collins and the Wartons, but Mallet and Akenside, show a distinct tendency to exalt the imagination and to emphasize its creative power, while Thomson, on the other hand, is more reserved.[31]   Mallet writes:

imagination is as much a part of reason as is memory or judgment, or rather a more bright emanation from it, as to paint and throw light on ideas is a finer act of understanding than simply to separate or compare them" (Leonard Welsted, *Concerning the Perfection of the English Language*, 1724).

[30]See *Critical Essays of the Eighteenth Century*, ed. W. H. Durham, New Haven, 1915, p. xxii.

[31]Among the critics influenced by Addison was Thomas Blackwell, whose *Enquiry into the Life and Writings of Homer* (1735) has so important a place in the evolution of eighteenth-century romantic theory. Blackwell quotes Addison with approval (p. 149). He finds that "imagination distinguishes the real poet, and one stroke of it

Companion of the muse, creative power,
Imagination! at whose great command
Arise unnumber'd images of things,
Thy hourly offspring: thou, who canst at will
People with air-born shapes the silent wood,
And solitary vale, thy own domain,
Where contemplation haunts; oh come, invok'd,
To waft me on thy many-tinctur'd wing,
O'er earth's extended space: and thence, on high,
Spread to superior worlds thy bolder flight,
Excursive, unconfin'd.[32]

Thomson, too, can talk of Shakespeare's 'creative fancy',[33] but it is clear that, in general, he regards nature as far transcending anything which the imagination can produce:

But who can paint
Like Nature?   Can imagination boast,

discovers him more than the greatest magnificence of words and pomp of description" (p. 148).   Nevertheless, it must merely adorn a body of truth, which is the prime necessity.   Blackwell, at bottom, adheres to the doctrine of imitation, in a manner similar to Thomson: "No imagination can supply the want of truth; flowery meads and horrid rocks, dismal dungeons and enchanted palaces, things all on extremes, can be easily imagined; but they take only with young and raw fancies, fit to be entertained with stories of dwarfs and distressed damsels. 'Tis the traces of truth that are irresistible, and the most fanciful fairy scene . . . . does not please like . . . . a prospect from the brow of the lofty Ide, because not real.   In the one the harmony established between the human understanding and truth commands our assent; in the other the mind wavers and views them passing like a waking dream" (pp. 285-6).

[32] *The Excursion*, Anderson's *British Poets*, IX, p. 688.

[33] *Summer*, l. 1564.   The phrase was added in the revision of 1744. With it Thomson couples a reference to Shakespeare's unrivalled powers of observation.

Amid its gay creation, hues like hers?
Or can it mix them with that matchless skill,
And lose them in each other, as appears
In every bud that blows?[34]—

questions which, pressed home, would throw the poet back
upon the imitation of nature alone; and indeed observation
and memory play a far larger part in Thomson's own
achievement than imagination in any extended sense.

To Akenside was left the task of versifying Addison's
theory as a whole. In *The Pleasures of Imagination* he
combines Addison on the imagination with much of
Shaftesbury on nature, art, and man, and he is long coming
to the place of the imagination in the act of artistic creation.
Memory, it appears, has been collecting and preserving her
'ideal train' of images:

> Thus at length
> Endow'd with all that nature can bestow,
> The child of Fancy oft in silence bends
> O'er these mixt treasures of his pregnant breast,
> With conscious pride. From them he oft resolves
> To frame he knows not what excelling things,
> And win he knows not what sublime reward
> Of praise and wonder. By degrees, the mind
> Feels her young nerves dilate; the plastic powers
> Labour for action; blind emotions heave
> His bosom; and with loveliest frenzy caught,
> From earth to heaven he rolls his daring eye,
> From heaven to earth. Anon ten thousand shapes,
> Like spectres trooping to the wizard's call,
> Flit swift before him. . . . .

[34] *Spring,* ll. 468-75.

> . . . . At length his plan
> Begins to open.   Lucid order dawns;
> And as from Chaos old the jarring seeds
> Of Nature at the voice divine repair'd
> Each to its place, till rosy earth unveil'd
> Her fragrant bosom, and the joyful sun
> Sprung up the blue serene; by swift degrees
> Thus disentangled, his entire design
> Emerges.   Colours mingle, features join,
> And lines converge: the fainter parts retire;
> The fairer, eminent in light, advance;
> And every image on its neighbour smiles.
> Awhile he stands, and with a father's joy
> Contemplates.   Then, with Promethean art,
> Into its proper vehicle he breathes
> The fair conception; which, embodied thus,
> And permanent, becomes to eyes or ears
> An object ascertain'd: while thus inform'd,
> The various organs of his mimic skill,
> The consonance of sounds, the featur'd rock,
> The shadowy picture and impassion'd verse,
> Beyond their proper powers attract the soul
> By that expressive semblance, while in sight
> Of Nature's great original we scan
> The lively child of Art; while line by line,
> And feature after feature, we refer
> To that sublime exemplar whence it stole
> Those animating charms.   Thus Beauty's palm
> Betwixt them wavering hangs; applauding Love
> Doubts where to choose; and mortal man aspires
> To tempt creative praise.[35]

[35]III, ll. 373-437, *Poet. Works*, ed. A. Dyce, Boston, 1864, pp. 179-81.

Here Akenside, without breaking loose from his Addisonian moorings or severing the connection between imagination and memory, proclaims in no uncertain terms the creative activity of the artist.

Joseph Warton, then, was not without contemporary precedent when he coined his ringing phrases on poetry and the creative imagination; nor was Collins entirely without such precedent when he proclaimed Heaven and Fancy "kindred powers."[36] In the preface to his *Odes* (1746), Joseph Warton declares "imagination and invention" to be "the chief faculties of a poet." In the dedication to Young[37] of his *Essay on Pope* (1756), he asserts that "it is a creative and glowing imagination and that alone" which makes the true poet, and in the body of the *Essay*, he writes:

"The 'man of rhymes' may be easily found; but the

[36]Further evidence of the degree to which these ideas were in the air is furnished by an anonymous essay, in Dodsley's *Museum* (1747, III, pp. 281-6), on the creative faculty of the poet, in which it is, in the true Renaissance manner, compared to God's, and by the anonymous ode, *The Pleasures of Poetry* (*Museum*, III, pp. 488-93).

[37]Young had an important subsidiary work to do for the full development of the theory of creative imagination, in attacking the imitation of models and advocating originality. Some of the leading contentions in his *Conjectures on Original Composition* (1759) are already present in his essay *On Lyric Poetry* (1728). Young himself is, as we have seen, extremely conservative in his attitude towards the imagination; but the idea of the creative imagination comes, in the latter half of the eighteenth century, to be associated with the cult of original genius. William Duff (*Essay on Original Genius*, 1767, pp. 6, 48, 262-3) finds that imagination is the dominant element in genius, more important than either judgment or taste, that, in short, "creative imagination" is "the distinguishing characteristic of true genius," and that of all the arts poetry is the most entirely dependent on that faculty.

genuine poet, of a lively plastic imagination, the true *maker* or *creator*, is so uncommon a prodigy, that one is almost tempted to subscribe to the opinion of Sir William Temple, where he says, 'that of all the numbers of mankind that live within the compass of a thousand years, for one man that is born capable of making a great poet, there may be a thousand born capable of making as great generals or ministers of state as the most renowned in story'."[38]

Despite his insistence on the creative imagination, one soon discovers in Warton the relics of other and divergent theories. Like Addison,[39] he maintains the emphasis on visual imagery and on the close association of imagination with memory.[40]   Like Thomson, he subordinates the idea of imagination to the doctrine of imitation, adding an all-too-characteristic touch of confusion, of his own.[41] Like all his immediate predecessors, he completely fails to arrive at any consistent theory of the imagination as an autono-

[38]*Essay on Pope*, London, 1806, I, pp. 108-9.

[39]Addison remains the most important influence on Warton, who praises his papers (*Essay on Pope*, I, p. 265) and repeats him and Akenside on greatness, novelty and beauty as the sources of the pleasures of the imagination (*Adventurer*, No. 80).

[40]He quotes Voltaire with approval: "He that retains the greatest number of images in the magazine of his memory has the best imagination;" and again: "The faculty of imagination depends entirely on memory. We see . . . . sensible objects; these perceptions enter the mind by our senses; the memory retains them; the imagination combines them; and this is the reason why the Greeks called the Muses the Daughters of Memory" (Pope, *Works*, ed. Joseph Warton, 1797, I, p. 183).

[41]"Thomson was blessed with a strong and copious fancy; he hath enriched poetry with a variety of new and original images, which he painted from nature itself and from his own actual observations" (*Essay on Pope*, I, p. 40).

mous power, shaping not the individual images merely, but the whole.[42]   The cautious historian will, of course, never look to the Wartons for consistent and thoroughgoing development of the ideas implicit in their own phrases.[43] Their romanticism was often more instinctive than self-conscious, and their historical importance lies mainly in their tendency to combine one part of revolutionary doctrine with three of orthodox platitude, and thus commend the whole compound to the readers of their day.

Joseph Warton's references to the poetic imagination are not confined to his critical writings.   Like Collins he has a poem on the subject, his *Ode to Fancy*,[44] and from it we may gather, better than from his prose, precisely what he

[42]Thomas Warton approaches more nearly to this concept.   Of *The Faery Queen* he writes: "If there be any poem whose graces please because they are situated beyond the reach of art, and where the force and faculties of creative imagination delight because they are unassisted and unrestrained by those of deliberate judgment, it is this" (*Observations on the Faery Queen*, London, 1820, I, pp. 23-4).   Here in connection with one of the dominant influences on the new poetry, the critic appears, for the time, to think of the imagination as no mere image-forming faculty, dependent on memory, but as capable of informing a whole work; he places creative imagination beyond the reach of conscious art, and he develops the antithesis of imagination and judgment (a mode of reason) in its romantic form.   This antithesis is, of course, also present in Joseph Warton.   He quotes with high approval, Bacon's distinction between the man of reason and the man of imagination (*Essay on Pope*, I, pp. 115-16); and this forms the basis not only of his own distinction between the poet and the man of wit and sense, but also of his remark, in the spirit of a later day: "Pope's close and constant reasoning had impaired and crushed the faculty of imagination. . . ." (*ibid.*, I, p. 276).

[43]See R. D. Havens. *Thomas Warton and the eighteenth-century Dilemma* (*Studies in Philol*. XXV, pp. 36 ff.).

[44]Chalmers's *English Poets*, XVIII, pp. 163-4.

expects of the faculty in its creative aspect. Fancy bears

> An all-commanding magic wand,
> Of pow'r to bid fresh gardens blow,
> 'Mid cheerless Lapland's barren snow.

In quest of her dwelling the poet wanders through various scenes. These are typical of the scenes which Fancy can create, and they range from romantic desolation to romantic beauty:

> Say, in what deep and pathless vale,
> Or on what hoary mountain's side,
> 'Mid fall of waters, you reside;
> 'Mid broken rocks, a rugged scene,
> With green and grassy dales between,
> 'Mid forests dark of aged oak. . . .
> Where Nature seems to sit alone
> Majestic on a craggy throne.

At last he will come where

> an hawthorne blows,
> Amid whose thickly-woven boughs
> Some nightingale still builds her nest,
> Each evening warbling thee to rest:
> Then lay me by the haunted stream,
> Rapt in some wild poetic dream,
> In converse while methinks I rove
> With Spenser through a fairy grove;
> Till, suddenly awak'd, I hear
> Strange whisper'd music in my ear,
> And my glad soul in bliss is drown'd
> By the sweetly-soothing sound!

The 'luxury of woe' is within Fancy's gift, with an accompaniment of 'gothic' terrors:

> Haste, Fancy, from the scenes of folly,
> To meet the matron Melancholy,
> Goddess of the tearful eye,
> That loves to fold her arms, and sigh;
> Let us with silent footsteps go
> To charnels and the house of woe,
> To Gothic churches, vaults, and tombs, . . .
> Or to some abbey's mould'ring tow'rs,
> Where, to avoid cold wintry show'rs,
> The naked beggar shivering lies,
> While whistling tempests round her rise,
> And trembles lest the tottering wall
> Should on her sleeping infants fall.

Not content with such mild emotions, the poet seeks stronger stimulants:

> 'Tis Fancy, in her fiery car,
> Transports me to the thickest war,
> There whirls me o'er the hills of slain,
> Where Tumult and Destruction reign;
> Where, mad with pain, the wounded steed
> Tramples the dying and the dead;
> Where giant Terror stalks around,
> With sullen joy surveys the ground,
> And, pointing to th' ensanguin'd field,
> Shakes his dreadful gorgon shield!

Enough has been quoted to show that for Warton, as for Collins, the function of the imagination is to create a romantic world of intenser experience, to supply scenes of ideal grandeur, beauty, wonder, terror.   In pursuit of this romantic world Warton was content that the imagination should fly beyond the limits of actual experience.   Witness his comment on *The Tempest*: "Of all the plays of Shakespeare, *The Tempest* is the most striking instance of his creative power.   He has there given the reins to his boundless imagination, and has carried the romantic, the wonderful, and the wild to the most pleasing extravagance."[45] With the Collins-Warton group, the imagination is to turn once more to what Bacon conceived to be her principal task, to create "a more ample greatness, a more exact goodness, and a more absolute variety than can be found in the nature of things."   That for them is the essence of the *creative imagination*.[46]

[45] *Adventurer*, No. 93.

[46] I have made no attempt to carry the discussion into the field of formal philosophy or to continue the history of *creative imagination* beyond Collins's day.   The reader will remember the dominant rôle assigned by Hume's *Treatise* to the faculty of imagination in the building up of knowledge, and will recognize that this, like the emphasis on sympathy in eighteenth-century ethics, is, in some measure, symptomatic of a gradual revolution in thought.   In connection with the later history of the idea he will recall what has been already said about the coalescence of the cult of *creative imagination* with that of *original genius*, and will further observe that in Blake we have the completion of that tendency, already apparent in Addison and emphatic in Collins and Joseph Warton, to think of the creative imagination as transcending nature.   Blake completely repudiates the association of imagination with memory and all efforts to divide her kingdom with nature and to regard poetry as merely an imaginative imitation of nature: "Natural objects always did and now do weaken, deaden, and obliterate imagination in me.   Wordsworth must know that what he writes valuable is not to be found in Nature."   He denounces (in his *Milton*) those

Who pretend to Poetry that they may destroy Imagination
By imitation of Nature's images drawn from remembrance.

III

It is our next task to observe in what respects the theories of the imagination canvassed above—not the idea of the creative imagination only but also the basic Addisonian theory—throw light on Collins's performance in his *Odes* (1746), and especially on the effects at which he aims.

Wherever the meagre relics of Collins permit us to institute a comparison, there emerges a striking parallel between his critical opinions and those of the Wartons.[1] Circumstances rendered abortive the project for the joint publication of Collins's and Joseph Warton's odes; but the significance of the project remains, and is enhanced by the fact that the two friends seem to have arranged at least for simultaneous publication.[2] We are, accordingly, on safe ground when we call in Warton's volume to supplement

He sums up his creed (*Ghost of Abel*):

Nature has no outline

But Imagination has. Nature has no tune, but Imagination has.

Nature has no supernatural and dissolves: Imagination is eternity. The antithesis between imagination and nature is broken down by Coleridge. Agreeing through "genial coincidence" with Schelling, he works out a metaphysical theory of "the shaping spirit of imagination", completes the task commenced by his eighteenth-century predecessors, and offers one, though certainly not the only possible solution for the two-fold problem of the relation of the poet's imaginings to nature and of their validity.

[1]After the question of the creative imagination, the most important of several examples is their advocacy of simplicity. Compare Collins's *Ode to Simplicity* with Joseph Warton's paper *On Simplicity in Taste* (*World*, No. 26).

[2]The project for joint publication dates, in all probability, from the early summer of 1746. It would appear that Dodsley accepted Warton's poems but refused those of Collins, who then found a publisher in Millar. The two volumes are listed successively in *The Gentleman's Magazine* for December, 1746.

our understanding of Collins's and when we assume that Warton's preface would probably have served to introduce the joint publication and have acted as the modest manifesto of the new school:[3]

"The public has been so much accustomed of late to didactic poetry alone, and essays on moral subjects, that any work where the *imagination* is much indulged will perhaps not be relished or regarded. The author, therefore, of these pieces is in some pain lest certain austere critics should think them too *fanciful* and *descriptive*. But as he is convinced that the fashion of moralizing in verse has been carried too far, and as he looks upon *invention* and *imagination* to be the *chief faculties of a poet*, so he will be happy if the following odes may be looked upon as an attempt to bring back poetry into its right channel."[4]

The relation of Collins and Warton to the poetry of their day is not our present concern. It may be observed, however, that the assertion regarding the prevalence of didactic or ethical verse would be borne out by a list of the chief publications in poetry between 1735 and 1750, including the contents of Dodsley's celebrated *Collection* (1748). The age sought its serious poetic reading not only in the *Moral Essays* and *Satires and Epistles* of Pope, but in the philosophical verse of Akenside, in the description, interspersed with reflection, of Thomson's *Seasons*,[5] in the art of pre-

[3]The youthful Thomas Warton, the third member of the group, was represented in his brother's volume by a translation from Horace, in the same metre as Collins's *Ode to Evening*.

[4]Quoted by Bronson, *op. cit.*, p. xxxix, n. 2.

[5]Thomson's effort had been to recall poetry to nature and to find therein food not only for "poetical enthusiasm" but for "philosophic reflection" (Preface to *Winter*, 2nd edition).

serving health, metrically expounded by Dr. Armstrong, or the art of producing wool, metrically expounded by Mr. Dyer, in the interminable moralizings of Young, and in the model of antique virtue, delineated, not without obvious pressings-home of the moral, by Richard Glover. Warton's subsequent praise of all the Pre-Romantics here listed makes it doubtful how far they are intended to fall under his condemnation; but that they deserve to do so there can be no doubt. For its amusement, as distinct from edification, the age found what it wanted in the lighter verses of Dodsley's *Collection* and other miscellanies, in rebus, epigram, Anacreontic, and similar trifles.[6] The allegorical ode, which does not emerge into any importance until the volumes of Collins and Warton,[7] is obviously a subdivision of what the eighteenth century called the *higher ode*, and the higher ode, belonging on the more serious level, tended to take on an ethical note, a fact witnessed by the odes of Akenside and Elizabeth Carter, as well as by the earlier odes of Gray. The opposition of Warton to this ethical trend is part of his protest against the commonplace and prosaic in verse, part of his demand for *pure poetry*, a concept and phrase in which he anticipates Mr. George Moore by a century and a half; and protest and demand alike are

[6]See R. D. Havens, *Changing Taste in the Eighteenth Century* (*P. M. L. A.*, XLIV, pp. 520 ff.).

[7]Emerging as a clearly recognizable form in the 1740's, it makes its way slowly. Not until the 1760's does it gain marked popularity, which it retains until about 1800. See R. D. Havens, *The Influence of Milton*, Cambridge (Mass.), 1922, pp. 441, 669-79. Mr. Havens's valuable "Bibliography II" contains only such poems as reveal the influence of Milton's companion pieces, but the number of allegorical odes in his list offers a fair indication of the popularity of the form.

made in the name of the creative imagination.[8]   While
bating no jot of belief in the poet's high calling and in the
dignity of his utterance, Collins and Warton turn from
moral reflection to 'invention' and 'description'.

It is necessary to draw out a little further the meaning
of these terms.   By the end of the eighteenth century
descriptive poetry meant primarily poetry of the type produced by Thomson and Cowper, the ethical-descriptive
poem.[9]   It is clear, however, that Collins and Warton
regarded the allegorical ode as forming an important branch
of descriptive poetry.[10]   Their own performance justifies

[8]The following passage from the *Essay on Pope* (I, pp. ii-iii) makes
clear the position taken up in the preface to the *Odes*: "We do not, it
should seem, sufficiently attend to the difference there is betwixt a man
of wit, a man of sense, and a true poet. . . . . Which of these characters
is the most valuable and useful is entirely out of the question: all I
plead for is to have their several provinces kept distinct from each
other; and to impress on the reader, that a clear head and acute understanding are not sufficient, alone, to make a poet; that the most solid
observations on human life, expressed with the utmost elegance and
brevity, are morality and not poetry; . . . . and that it is a creative
and glowing imagination, *acer spiritus ac vis*, and that alone that can
stamp a writer with this exalted and very uncommon character. . . ."

[9]In 1797, Mrs. Barbauld questions the propriety of the term "descriptive" in Collins's title.

[10]As early as 1738, Henry Pemberton's *Observations on Poetry* class-
ified the ode as a form of descriptive poem.   Newbery's *Art of Poetry
on a New Plan* (1761) treats as descriptive poetry not the ode itself,
but *L'Allegro* and *Il Penseroso*, among the most important formative
influences on it, commenting on their "beautiful use of the figure called
prosopopœia."   Richard Shepherd speaks of the *descriptive* and
allegorical ode as one of the recognized forms of modern poetry (*Odes
Descriptive and Allegorical*, 1761).   John Ogilvie observes that "a
certain picturesque vivacity of description" is "characteristic of the
ode" (*Poems on Several Subjects*, 1762).

this opinion. Not only do they, on occasion, blend with their extensive use of personification some measure of landscape description, in the general manner anticipated in Milton's companion pieces and in Dyer's *Grongar Hill*, but they habitually treat the personifications themselves in a descriptive and highly pictorial way. The fact demands emphasis: in Warton, and more especially in Collins, the allegorical *is* the descriptive. Their personifications have nothing in common with those condemned by Coleridge: they are not of the 'printer's devil' variety, with no sign of life but the capital letter. They are not introduced as counters in a game of ethical platitudes, but as occasions for pictorial description. They are not, as is so often assumed, a relic of Augustan convention; they are, at the very least, a fresh and vigorous device for lending animation to the lyric.

In Collins's odes, the 'persons', though rarely described in much detail, are hardly ever without their vivid descriptive epithet or phrase, and they are nearly always placed in a setting. The suggestive and eminently visual character of the phrasing compensates for its brevity. The result is a word-picture whose effect approximates to that of an allegorical painting or, more exactly, the sketch for an allegorical picture. For example, Collins addresses Peace:

> O thou who bad'st thy turtles bear
> Swift from his grasp thy golden hair,
>   And sought'st thy native skies:
> When War, by vultures drawn from far,
> To Britain bent his iron car,
>   And bad his storm arise.[11]

[11] *Ode to Peace*, ll. 1-6.

One cannot doubt that the effect sought is almost wholly
pictorial. The stanza is like a sketch of some allegorical
painting by Rubens. Its features could be catalogued
precisely as could those of such a painting: On the right
is the male figure War, borne through the air in an iron
chariot, which is drawn by vultures and supported on dark
storm-clouds; before him rises the female figure Peace,
ascending to the heavens, with her doves circling around
her; War is reaching forward to grasp her tresses, which
are brushed from his hand by the doves; in the distance,
beneath the storm-clouds, appears the isle of Britain,
towards which War's flight is directed. Some of the details
are, of course, but slightly suggested, and nothing is described minutely; but no one, I fancy, can fail to see that
it is the effect of the allegorical painter that Collins is trying
to rival. This effect occurs repeatedly in the volume of
1746:

> But O how alter'd was its sprightlier tone
> When *Cheerfulness, a nymph of healthiest hue,*
>   *Her bow across her shoulders flung,*
>   *Her buskins gemm'd with morning dew,*
> *Blew an inspiring air,* that *dale and thicket* rung,
>   The hunter's call to faun and dryad known!
> *The oak-crown'd sisters and their chaste-ey'd queen,*
>   *Satyrs and sylvan boys were seen,*
>   *Peeping from forth their alleys green;*
> *Brown Exercise* rejoic'd to hear,
>   *And Sport leapt up and seized his beechen spear.*[12]

The Passions is supposed to be descriptive of music, but in
truth it is a series of pictures. Or take, as a final example,

[12] *The Passions*, ll. 69-79.

the lines depicting the single figure Pity, which eighteenth-century criticism[13] singled out for their pictorial effect:

> Long, Pity, let the nations view
> Thy sky-worn robes of tend'rest blue
> And eyes of dewy light![14]

Here it is not Rubens but Raphael of whom one involuntarily thinks.[15]

In elaborating their pictorial effects, Collins and Warton are influenced in part by literary models, by Spenser, by the minor poems of Milton, by the earlier writings of Pope,[16]

[13]Daniel Webb, *Observations on the Correspondence between Poetry and Music*, London, 1769, pp. 133-6.

[14]*Ode to Pity*, ll. 10-12.

[15]Collins, the most uneven of poets, frequently, of course, falls below the level of these passages. Other instances of similar pictorial effects are: *Pity* ll. 1-6; *Fear* ll. 10-23, 48-51; *Mercy*, ll. 1-6, 7-10; *To a Lady* ll. 1-6, 19-24, 41-2 (together with one suppressed stanza of 1746 and two of 1747); *Peace*, ll. 13-18, 19-24; *Manners*, ll. 13-18, 54-8; *Passions* ll. 29-38, 40-53, 57-65, 89-94.

[16]Of *Windsor Forest* ll. 413-22, Warton writes (*Essay on Pope*, I, pp. 27-8): "The group of allegorical personages. . .are worthy of the pencil of Rubens or Julio Romano: it may, perhaps, however, be wished that the epithets *barbarous* (Discord), *mad* (Ambition), *hateful* (Envy) had been particular and picturesque, instead of general and indiscriminating; though it may possibly be urged, that in describing the dreadful inhabitants of the portal of hell, Virgil has not always used such adjuncts and epithets as a painter or statuary might work after. . . . . I make no scruple of adding, that in this famous passage, Virgil has exhibited no images so lively and distinct as these living figures painted by Pope, each of them with their proper insignia and attributes."

and possibly by one or two other poets;[17] but beyond these, I think, one may safely assume a direct influence from the pictorial arts themselves. The Horatian phrase *ut pictura poesis* had long been firmly embedded in the Neo-classical theory of poetry. It was felt to have special application to the descriptive poem, and the landscape poets, perhaps the most important group among the Pre-Romantics, were unquestionably led to challenge the painter's effects and to draw extensively on such well-known artists as Salvator Rosa and Claude Lorrain:[18] in the early Pre-Romantics one already commences to recognize the cult of the picturesque.[19] The descriptive and allegorical ode, within its more confined limits, challenged similar effects and presumably responded to similar influences. It found ready to its hand an abundance of pictorial allegory, in the painters from Raphael to Rubens and beyond, and in the engravers, and in collections or reproductions of ancient medals.[20]

[17]*E.g.*, John Hughes. *Cf.* his *Essay on Allegorical Poetry* (1715), where he remarks: "The resemblance which has been so often observed in general between poetry and painting is yet more particular in allegory, which . . . . is a kind of picture in poetry." Such ethical-descriptive poets as Collins's friends Thomson and John Gilbert Cooper also occasionally and faintly parallel his effects in the use of personification.

[18]See E. W. Manwaring, *Italian Landscape in Eighteenth-century England*, New York, 1925.

[19]See C. Hussey, *The Picturesque*, London, 1927.

[20]Spence's *Polymetis* (1747) is typical of the interest of students of ancient art and literature in the personifications represented on medals. To the suggestion that if an artist would excel, he should study Polymetis' collection, Polymetis replies: "You are right . . . . and it would not be at all amiss if you would send your poets thither too: I mean, only to form their ideas as to the imaginary or allegorical per-

Besides the descriptive treatment of his allegorical figures, Collins's odes contain other pictorial effects:—the unforgettable Spartan youths,[21] the idealized landscape of the *Ode to Evening*, the poetic paradise of Milton:

> High on some cliff, to heav'n up-pil'd,
> Of rude access, of prospect wild,
> Where, tangled round the jealous steep,
> Strange shades o'er-brow the valleys deep,
> And holy genii guard the rock,
> Its glooms embrown, its springs unlock,
> While on its rich ambitious head
> An Eden, like his own, lies spread . . . .[22]

True there is little accurate detail as compared with a descriptive poet like Thomson; but every word is directed to the imagination of the reader. Finally, besides these larger word-pictures, Collins's odes abound in bright visual images, residing in a single word or phrase, and sometimes crowded together within the space of a few lines:

> Beyond yon *braided clouds* that lie
> Paving the *light-embroider'd* sky,
> Amidst the bright *pavilion'd* plains. . . . .[23]

sonages which they may have occasion to introduce into their poems." The whole question demands more detailed treatment than the bald summary which my space permits. For example, one should not neglect the vogue of personification in the prose essay. Collins, thanking his friend Cooper for an essay contributed to his projected journal, says, "It is my sincere opinion that the subject could not have been treated in any more *picturesque* or forcible allegory" (*London Mercury*, XI, p. 173).

[21] *Ode to Liberty* ll. 1-6.
[22] *Ode on the Poetical Character*, ll. 55-62.
[23] *Ode to Liberty*, ll. 103-5.

It is in virtue of these effects that Collins (in his title) and Warton (in the preface) term the odes *descriptive*. In their conscious effort to call poetry back to the walks of imagination, they concentrate upon descriptive writing, and they seek to fill their verses with visual imagery. Addison had viewed the imagination as a faculty whose chief function was the compounding of visual images; he had dwelt on the place of imagination, thus conceived, in descriptive writing, and had equated the effects of such writing with those of painting and statuary.[24] This view of the imagination persisted despite the increasing emphasis on the faculty's inventive or creative power. It was accepted by Warton, and presumably by Collins. Their talk of the creative imagination should not blind us to the fact that Addison's basic theory still exercised its influence upon their minds. With this theory Collins's odes, in some of their major aspects, are in perfect harmony. They are descriptive and imaginative in the sense in which these closely-linked terms were understood.

They are also imaginative in a larger sense, by virtue of the *invented* material with which they deal: they depict things out of nature and must create the objects which they describe. It remains, then, to develop the implications in Warton's term 'invention' and to suggest the relation of Collins's odes to their jointly-held theory of the creative imagination. When Warton spoke of personification as "one of the greatest efforts of the creative power of a warm and lively imagination,"[25] he was no doubt uttering an opinion which Collins shared. Indeed the idea is already

[24] *Spectator*, Nos. 411, 416.
[25] *Adventurer*, No. 57.

implicit in Addison and in the pioneer of Spenserian studies, John Hughes.

Addison—and the fact has a further significance for the student of Collins—treats personification in close connection with 'the fairy way of writing' and regards the two as a field for the imagination in its most creative moments:

"There is a kind of writing wherein *the poet quite loses sight of nature* and entertains his reader's imagination with the characters and actions of such persons as have many of them no existence but what he bestows on them. Such are fairies, witches, magicians, demons, and departed spirits. This Mr. Dryden calls 'the fairy way of writing,' which is indeed more difficult than any other that depends 'on the poet's fancy, because he has no pattern to follow in it, and *must work altogether out of his own invention.* . . .

"*These descriptions raise a pleasing kind of horror in the mind of the reader and amuse his imagination with the strangeness and novelty* of the persons who are represnted to them. *They . . . favour those secret terrors and apprehensions to which the mind of man is naturally subject.*[26] We are pleased with surveying the different habits and behaviours of foreign countries: how much more must we be delighted and surprised when we are led, as it were, into a new creation. . . . .

"There is another sort of imaginary beings that we sometimes meet with among the poets, when the author represents any passion, appetite, virtue or vice under a visible shape, and makes it a person or an actor in his poem. Of this nature are the descriptions of Hunger and Envy in Ovid, of Fame in Virgil, and of Sin and Death in Milton.

[26]*Cf.* Collins's *Ode to Fear*, ll. 54-63.

We find a whole creation of like shadowy persons in Spenser, who had an admirable talent in representations of this kind. . . . . Thus we see how many ways poetry addresses itself to the imagination, as it has not only the whole circle of nature for its province but makes new worlds of its own, shows us persons who are not to be found in being, and represents even the faculties of the soul, with the several virtues and vices, in a sensible shape and character."[27]

These ideas are elaborated by John Hughes. Writing of allegorical poetry,[28] with special reference to Spenser, he remarks: "Allegory is indeed the fairy-land of poetry, peopled by imagination; *its inhabitants are so many apparitions. . . .*" In its strictest meaning, it presents only "fictitious persons or beings, creatures of the poet's brain, and actions *surprising* and *without the bounds of probability or nature.*" As it "sometimes introduces creatures which are out of nature, as goblins, chimæras, fairies, and the like, so it *frequently gives life to virtues and vices,* passions and diseases, to *natural and moral qualities,* and *represents them acting as divine, human,* or *infernal persons.*" In short, as there is "more invention employed in a work of this kind than in mere narration . . . . it consequently requires a more than ordinary heat of fancy in its first production."

In the decade after Collins wrote we encounter the phrase *creative description.* The critic is discriminating between various types of descriptive writing. One presents "objects that never at all exist but in the poet's imagination, as Homer's gods and goddesses, the Muses, fairies, genii of

[27] *Spectator,* No. 419.

[28] *Essay on Allegorical Poetry* (1715). The passages quoted are from *Critical Essays of the Eighteenth Century,* pp. 91, 92, 95, 99.

places, the virtues and vices personified, and other branches of the poetical machinery, which I beg leave to call creative description."[29]   It is clear that in the criticism of Addison, Hughes, and Warton, and in the performance of Collins, this conception is already fully developed.   Thus it is that Warton can designate his own odes and (we have seen reason to believe) those of Collins, as predominantly imaginative,—that is, marked at once by "invention" and "description".   Thus it is, moreover, that Collins, working within the limits of the descriptive and allegorical ode, as he and his group understand it, can produce such striking romantic effects as that achieved in his address to Fear:

> Thou to whom the world unknown
> With all its shadowy shapes is shown;
> Who see'st appall'd th' unreal scene,
> *While Fancy lifts the veil between* . . . .
> For lo what monsters in thy train appear!
> Danger, whose limbs of giant mold
> What mortal eye can fix'd behold?
> Who stalks his round, an hideous form,
> Howling amidst the midnight storm,
> Or throws him on the ridgy steep
> Of some loose hanging rock to sleep:
> And with him thousand phantoms join'd,
> Who prompt to deeds accurs'd the mind:
> And those, the fiends who, near allied,
> O'er Nature's wounds and wrecks preside;
> While Vengeance in the lurid air
> Lifts her red arm, expos'd and bare . . . .[30]

[29]Robert Andrews's *Eidyllia*, Edinburgh, 1759.
[30]*Ode to Fear*, ll. 1-21.

Collins, it would seem, conceives his "persons" as creatures of the spirit-world. They are revealed to him in a
sort of vision. With them move other visitants from the
same regions, the demons who preside over nature's cataclysms and mankind's crimes.[31]   And the result, for the poet,

³¹There are two allusions in Collins to these spirits, who, apparently
dwell in the elements and preside over storm and earthquake as well as
over human violence. No attempt has ever been made to explain
their meaning or to find their source.

It seems that in the last lines quoted above we have a fairly distinct
echo of that devil-lore which found a limited place in Renaissance
literature, of which there is a hint in Lady Macbeth's appeal to the
spirits who "tend on mortal thoughts"

> (. . . . you murdering ministers,
> Wherever in your sightless substances
> You wait on nature's mischief),

and of which the *locus classicus* in English literature is, of course, in
Nashe's *Pierce Penniless his Supplication to the Devil*. Nashe gives
an elaborate account of the spirits who incense men to deeds of violence
and iniquity, and with them he couples the Spirit of Revenge, who in
Collins's lines is likewise present, in the form of the personified Ven-
geance: "The second kind of devils . . . . are those Northern Marcii
. . . . *the authors of massacres and seedsmen of mischief; for they have
commission to incense men to rapines, sacrilege*, theft, *murder*, wrath,
fury, and all manner of cruelties, and they command certain of the
Southern Spirits as slaves, to wait upon them, as also great Arioch, that
is termed the *Spirit of Revenge*" (*Works*, ed. R. B. McKerrow, London,
1904-8, p. 230). In the lines quoted from *Macbeth*, "nature" from the
context would appear to mean human nature. Nashe, however, proceeds immediately to a class of fiends who operate in nature itself and
do their deadly work through storm and earthquake: "Therefore are
they counted the most pestilent, troublesome, and guileful spirits that
are; for *by help of* Alrynach, *a spirit of the West, they will raise storms,
cause earthquakes*, whirlwinds, rain, hail or snow. . .The spirits of the air
will mix themselves with thunder and lightning" (*ibid.*, I, p. 231). Here,
as in Collins's lines, are fiends who prompt or incense the minds of men

is a new creation, a world of ideal wonder, touched with terror. Or again, in another mood, it is a world of ideal beauty and tranquillity that he creates, where gracious figures from classic myth and the elves of native folklore join with the beautiful forms, the children of his own brain:

to "deeds accursed", and, associated with them, are spirits who preside over the cataclysms of nature, and the *Spirit of Revenge*. Though there is no similarity of phrasing—that one would not expect — there is a striking similarity of very uncommon content. Our knowledge of Collins's interests and of his eager, unsystematic reading in Renaissance literature (which we owe to his poems and to Thomas Warton's *History of English Poetry*) makes it seem not at all improbable that at some time he had perused Nashe's book.

In the *Ode to Liberty* (ll. 73-4), Collins commences his account of storm and earthquake with a cryptic phrase. Britain and Gaul were joined

Till all *the banded West* at once '*gan rise,*

A wide wild storm, ev'n Nature's self confounding. . . . .

What is the *banded West?* No one knows. I suggest that Collins is thinking of a group of spirits associated with the West and banded together for the production of storm and earthquake, and that here we have a memory (slightly inaccurate as such memories are apt to be in Collins) of the second passage quoted from Nashe, with its talk of the spirits who produce these cataclysms of nature by the aid of the spirit of the West.

A third passage, in the *Ode to Mercy* (ll. 14-16), contains a reference to the Fiend of Nature, which has baffled commentators. One would not readily sacrifice Bronson's suggestion that the passage is an allusion to the Jacobite invasion of 1745. Remembering Nashe's account of the spirits in nature who preside over "massacres, murder, fury, and all manner of cruelties", such as are attendant on civil war, one fancies that Bronson's explanation may be correct, and, further, that the source of Collins's image may be the devil-lore of Nashe.

For when thy folding-star arising shows
His paley circlet, at his warning lamp
    The fragrant Hours, and elves
    Who slept in flow'rs the day,

And many a nymph who wreathes her brows with sedge,
And sheds the fresh'ning dew, and lovelier still,
    The pensive Pleasures sweet
    Prepare thy shadowy car. . . . .[32]

The lightness of Collins's touch and the art which so frequently subdues mere thrills to the larger purposes of
beauty, are apt to conceal from all but the careful reader the
essentially romantic elements of which his allegorical
imagery is compounded or with which it is combined.
Take, for example, the passing suggestion of the "gothic"
note in the "ruin midst the dreary dells" to which Evening
is to lead her votary, or the combination of images which
serves to add a suggestion of the mediaeval, as well as of
fairy lore and the world of benign spirits, to his loveliest
lines:

    By *fairy hands* their knell is rung;
    By *forms unseen* their dirge is sung;
    There *Honour* comes, *a pilgrim grey*,
    To bless the turf that wraps their clay,
    And Freedom shall awhile repair,
    To dwell a weeping *hermit* there![33]

Sometimes the spirits hover in the background but still add
to the scene a vague note of old romance:

[32]*Ode to Evening*, ll. 21-8.
[33]*Ode written in 1746*, ll. 7-12.

With eyes uprais'd, as one inspir'd,
Pale Melancholy sate retir'd,
And from her wild sequester'd seat,
In notes by distance made more sweet,
Pour'd thro' the mellow horn her pensive soul:
And dashing soft from rocks around,
Bubbling runnels join'd the sound;
Thro' glades and glooms the mingled measure stole,
Or *o'er some haunted stream* with fond delay . . .[34]

Even where the note of the supernatural is absent, Collins's personifications assume a visionary quality. Pity is a figure hovering in the heavens, at which the nations gaze. Mercy is a native of the skies:

O thou who sitt'st a smiling bride
By Valour's arm'd and awful side,
Gentlest of sky-born forms, and best ador'd . . .[35]

And around the twilight tomb of Ross,

Aerial forms shall sit at eve
And bend the pensive head!
And, fall'n to save his injur'd land,
Imperial Honour's awful hand
Shall point his lonely bed.[36]

Here one has writing which is imaginative not merely in the restricted sense of being pictorial, but in the larger sense of being inventive or creative. For Collins the allegorical, descriptively treated, provides, temporarily, the mode in which invention or the creative imagination can

[34] *The Passions*, ll. 57-65.
[35] *Ode to Mercy*, ll. 1-3.
[36] *Ode to a Lady*, ll. 20-4.

best operate. It offers free play to his imagination by
allowing him to create his own world of ideal forms. The
very remoteness of this new world from that actual world
on which the Neo-classical poets had largely concentrated,
is for him its peculiar charm; and this fact, apart from the
specific contents of his world, marks it as romantic and
Collins's imagination as of the romantic or idyllic order.
Instinctively the poet rebels against the limitations of
actual experience. Like Warton he desires to achieve
through invention or the creative imagination a field of
freer and more intense experience, visions of a more absolute
beauty, variety, and wonder than the actual world can
afford.

Johnson has characterized Collins's imagination once for
all, and has placed in its proper relation the allegorical
imagery of the odes:

"He had employed his mind chiefly upon works of fiction
and subjects of fancy, and by indulging some peculiar habits
of thought, was *eminently delighted with those flights of
imagination which pass the bounds of nature* and to which the
mind is reconciled only by a passive acquiescence in popular
traditions. He loved fairies, genii, giants, and monsters;
he delighted to rove through the meanders of enchantment,
to gaze on the magnificence of golden palaces, to repose by
the waterfalls of Elysian gardens. . . . . (T)he grandeur of
wildness and the novelty of extravagance were always
desired by him. . . . . This idea which he had formed of
excellence led him to oriental fictions and *allegorical imagery. . . . .*"[37]

[37] *Works*, New York, 1851, II, pp. 275-6.   For the moment I suppress
Johnson's judgment on the success which crowns Collins's efforts: our
concern is with his aims.

Beside this masterly analysis it is instructive to place a passage from one of the most celebrated modern essays on Romanticism. In *The Renascence of Wonder*, Watts-Dunton comments on the striking picture of Danger in the *Ode to Fear*, quoted above:

"And again who had a finer imagination than Collins? Who possessed more fully than he the imaginative power of seeing a man asleep on a loose hanging rock, and of actualizing in a dramatic way the peril of the situation? But there is something very ungenteel about a mere man, as Augustanism had discovered. A man is a very homely and common creature, and the worker in polite letters must avoid the homely and the common; whereas a personification of Danger is literary, Augustan, and 'polite.' Hence Collins, having first imagined with excessive vividness a man hanging on a loose rock asleep, set to work immediately to turn the man into an abstraction."

Nothing could be more determinedly wrong-headed. For Collins's Danger is not a man, but a giant being whom no "mortal eye can fix'd behold"; in the whole passage under discussion we have the first vintage of the poet's imagination and not an artificial product, prepared for a market which, in all probability, never existed. Danger is a figure of ideal wonder touched with terror, the creature of a shadowy spirit world, revealed to the poet in a sort of vision while "fancy lifts the veil between." And so with the "persons" of the other odes, ideal forms of pathos, of beauty, or of wonder, they are the products of the creative imagination, and for the poet, at least, they have their own peculiar kind of reality. Was not Truth present when the magic girdle was weaving, along with Wonder and "the shadowy

tribes of mind"? Undoubtedly Collins's personifications
are the figures of an age as well as ideal forms; but their
relation to the age is not the absurdly simple one that
Watts-Dunton (typical of a whole tradition in criticism)
supposes. It is a relation which can be made clear only
by a study of the *Odes* in close connection with their critical
background and especially in connection with the shifting
concept of "imagination".

Into the limitations inherent in the allegorical method
there is no need to go: they are obvious enough. Up to a
certain point, however, it served Collins well. Besides
giving him a vehicle for the type of effects which he was,
perhaps, best fitted to achieve, it ministered occasion for
further explorations in the realm of his own imagining and
for the harvesting of results. It is in connection with the
progress of the goddess Liberty to "her lov'd, her last abode"
that he is led into his account of the severing of Britain from
Gaul, perhaps the most spirited piece of romantic verse
between Milton and Coleridge:

> Beyond the measure vast of the thought,
>   The works the wizard Time hath wrought!
> The Gaul, 'tis held in antique story,
>   Saw Britain link'd to his now adverse strand;
> No sea between, nor cliff sublime and hoary,
> He pass'd with unwet feet through all our land.
>   To the blown Baltic then, they say,
>   The wild waves found another way,
> Where Orcas howls, his wolfish mountains rounding;
>   Till all the banded West at once 'gan rise,
> A wide wild storm, ev'n Nature's self confounding,

With'ring her giant sons with strange uncouth
  surprise.
  This pillar'd earth so firm and wide,
    By winds and inward labours torn,
  In thunders dread was push'd aside,
    And down the should'ring billows borne.
And see, like gems, her laughing train,
  The little isles on ev'ry side!
Mona, once hid from those who search the main,
  Where thousand elfin shapes abide,
And Wight, who checks the west'ring tide;
  For thee consenting Heav'n has each bestowed,
A fair attendant on her sov'reign pride.
  To thee this blest divorce she ow'd,
For thou hast made her vales thy lov'd, thy last
  abode![38]

What, apart from memories of pictorial personifications
in Spenser, in Milton, and in the allegorical painters, are
the materials with which Collins's imagination works? The
originality of his total effects has resulted in some tendency
to overlook the part which literary reminiscence, conscious
or unconscious, plays in his odes. Already in 1782, his
originality of image was commencing to be contrasted with
Gray's studious borrowing; [39] and the labour of a long succession of able commentators from Dyce and Mitford to
Mr. Garrod has not served wholly to dissipate the impression thus early recorded. An investigation of the sources
and analogues of the passage last quoted will offer a partial
answer to the question regarding the materials with which

[38]*Ode to Liberty*, ll. 64-88.
[39]*Gentleman's Magazine*, LII, pp. 20-1.

the poet's imagination works, and may incidentally contribute its mite to the definitive edition of Collins which must some day be made. The reader with no taste for the deadly parallel has received due warning and may discreetly skip the ensuing paragraph.

In a footnote to line 67, Collins vaguely remarks that the connection of Britain and Gaul is a tradition "mentioned by several of our older historians"[40] but that to the best of his knowledge no "poetical use has been hitherto made of it".[41]   The work on which Collins appears to have drawn most largely is Camden's *Britannia*.[42]   In his footnote Collins comments on "the correspondent disposition of the opposite coasts", and in the text writes of the "cliff sublime and hoary" (l. 68).   Camden observes that "the shore of either side, where the distance between is narrowest, riseth up with lofty cliffs of the same matter as it were, and colour."   Camden suggests that the division occurred by the "rushing in of the waves or else by occasion of some earthquake"; and Collins (ll. 76-9) adopts both sugges-

[40]*Cf.* Selden's *Illustrations of Drayton's Polyolbion*, a work which, however, Collins was, apparently, not at first-hand familiar.

[41]I think that we must accept this statement as made in good faith, and indeed there is no more than a glancing reference to the tradition in Drayton's *Polyolbion*, song xviii, ll. 718-20.   Collins's boast is parodied in a note to the *Ode to Horror* (H. O. White, in *T. L. S.*, 1922, p. 28).   A plausible explanation of error and jest alike might be that Collins had been directed to the historians by his antiquarian friends the Wartons, and had carelessly overlooked the poetical passage in connection with which the historians had been mentioned.   If, as I have suggested (*T.L.S.*, 1929, pp. 62, 420), Thomas Warton should turn out to be the anonymous author of the *Ode to Horror*, this hypothesis would completely cover the facts.

[42]My quotations are from Philemon Holland's translation (*Britain*, London, 1610, pp. 346-7).

tions. Camden quotes Virgil's reference to the separation of Sicily and Italy,

> Tantum aevi longinqua valet mutare vetustas;[43]

and a similar phrase strikes the keynote of Collins's anti-strophe (ll. 64-5). Nor is Camden without his sense of the wonder and terror of these cataclysms in nature,[44] the aspect seized upon by Collins. With these suggestions from Camden as its point of departure the poet's imagination weaves its tissue of romantic suggestion, drawing on other stores of memory, here for a thought and there for a phrase. The introduction of myth and the manner of it (l. 66) are Pindaric.[45] Collins's memories of Spenser were apt to be more vivid than accurate,[46] and it is not impossible that the image in line 69 was suggested by Spenser's phrase, occurring in another mythological context:

> Out of his Albion did on dry-foot pas
> Into old Gall.[47]

The striking line on Orcas (l. 72) is an obvious reminiscence of Pope, incongruous though the context of the image in that poet be:

[43]*Aeneid*, III, l. 415, briefly rendered by Holland, "Such change makes time."

[44]Quoting from Seneca, he says: "You see there is a separation made both of countries and nations when as some part of nature is provoked of itself or when the mighty wind beateth strongly upon some sea; the force whereof as in general is wonderful. For although it rage but in part, yet it is of the universal power that it so rageth."

[45]*Cf.* Pindar's *Olympian Odes*, vii ("But the tale is told in antique story how that Zeus," *etc.*, trans. Sandys).

[46]See Bronson's note on *Ode on the Poetical Character*, l. 5.

[47]*Faery Queen*, IV, xi, 16, 3-4.

> Loud as the wolves on Orcas' stormy steep
> Howl to the roarings of the northern deep.[48]

As I have already observed, no attempt has ever been made to explain the lines introducing Collins's account of storm and earthquake (ll. 73-4) with their cryptic allusion to "the banded West"; it may be that they are another reference to the demons of nature described in Nashe's *Pierce Penniless*.[49] The giant inhabitants of pre-historic Britain (l. 75) are mentioned by Camden.[50] The actual phrase "giant sons" occurs in Milton,[51] and the rest of the line strangely echoes Dryden's image: "and *wild amazement . . . withers* even the strong."[52] The idea of earthquake and storm as the cause of separation (ll. 76-9) comes, as we have seen, from Camden. Elaborating the hint, Collins adopts the explanation of earthquakes current in the sixteenth and seventeenth centuries.[53] Perhaps he remembers how Milton has used it, coupling earthquake and the rush of waters:

> Winds underground and waters forcing way
> Sidelong have pushed a mountain from his seat.[54]

Perhaps this memory led by swift, unconscious association

---

[48]*To Augustus*, ll. 328-9.

[49]It is unnecessary to repeat the argument here; see above, note 31.

[50]*Britain*, p. 5. Bronson's suggestion of Geoffrey of Monmouth as the source becomes, therefore, superfluous.

[51]*Par. Lost* I, l. 778, whence it was borrowed by Thomson (*Autumn*, l. 803).

[52]*Palamon and Arcite*, III, ll. 302-3.

[53]See for example Gabriel Harvey's account of an earthquake in the second of his *Three Proper and Witty Familiar Letters*, and *Par. Lost* I, ll. 230-3, VI, ll. 195-8.

[54]*Par. Lost*, VI, ll. 196-7.

to another—the same poet's description of desperate storms
(which seem "as earth and sky would mingle"):

> mortals fear them
> As dangerous to the *pillared* frame of heaven
> And to the *earth's* dark basis underneath.[55]

And so on to Spenser, his second favourite,[56] where we find
the hint for the "should'ring billows":

> Eftsoons of thousand billows shouldred.[57]

It is by some such processes that Collins learns and incor-
porates the great language of his masters.   The gem-like
isles (ll. 80-1) are a palpable reminiscence of *Comus*:

> all the sea-girt isles
> That, like rich and various gems, inlay
> The unadorned bosom of the deep.[58]

The allusions to Mona (ll. 82-3) are almost certainly
memories of Collins's reading in George Waldron's *History
and Description of the Isle of Man*, of which a third edition
was issued in 1744.   There he would find an abundance of

---

[55]*Par. Regained*, IV, ll. 454-6; *cf. Comus*, l. 598 and *Par. Lost*, IX
l. 1106; the epithet is borrowed from Milton by Thomson (*Autumn*,
l. 134).

[56]My investigations of Collins's imagery lead me to suppose that
Milton is by far the most frequent source.   Of the remaining sources
the order appears to be somewhat as follows: Spenser, Thomson, Pope,
Shakespeare, Fairfax's translation of Tasso's *Jerusalem Delivered*,
Dryden, with very occasional borrowings from others, amongst them
the Wartons and Akenside.

[57]*Ruins of Rome*, l. 213; *cf.* also *sea-shouldring* (*Faery Queen*, II,
xii, 23. 6) which Keats was later to admire.

[58]Ll. 21-3 (Dyce).

supernatural wonders and a comment on the belief, wide-spread among the natives, "that there is not a creek or cranny in this island but what is haunted either with fairies or ghosts."[59]   Hence the allusion to "thousand elfin shapes."   In Waldron Collins would also read:

"Some hundred years, say they, before the coming of our Saviour, the Isle of Man was inhabited by a certain species called fairies, and that everything was carried on in a kind of supernatural manner; that a blue mist hanging contin-ually over the land, prevented the ships that passed by from having any suspicion there was an island."[60]

Here, then, is the probable source of Collins's allusion to "Mona once hid from those who search the main."[61]

[59]*History and Description of the Isle of Man*, London, 1744, pp. 132-3.
[60]*Ibid.*, p. 14.
[61]Collins's text presents no difficulty. His footnote is, however, a dark saying, and seems to point to a tradition quite different from that recorded by Waldron, whom I have assumed to be his source.   Collins writes: "There is a tradition in the Isle of Man, that a mermaid, becoming enamour'd of a young man of extraordinary beauty, took an opportunity of meeting him one day as he walk'd on the shore, and open'd her passion to him, but was received with a coldness, occasion'd by his horror and surprise at her appearance. This, however, was so misconstru'd by the sea-lady that, in revenge for his treatment of her, she punish'd the whole island by covering it with a mist, so that all who attempted to carry on any commerce with it either never arriv'd at it, but wander'd up and down the sea, or were on a sudden wreck'd upon its cliffs."   No such tradition as the one to which Collins refers is known. A second tradition there is (unmentioned by Waldron) which attributes the mist to the Irish magician Manannan, whose wicked charm was broken by St. Patrick; but this is clearly nothing to our purpose. Now Waldron does record the traditional story of a mermaid who fell in love with a mortal, with which up to a certain point Collins's agrees: "A very beautiful mermaid, say they, became

Finally, with the unusual epithet "westering" (l. 84) we return to Milton.[62]

One does not suppose, of course, that this attempt to run down the sources of Collins's imagery is complete or that its findings are all on the same level of probability; one would not for a moment suggest that the reminiscences are all conscious; but one may, I think, claim a general and approximate accuracy for the whole. The processes which the investigation reveals are thoroughly character-

so much enamour'd of a young man who used to tend his sheep on these rocks, that she would frequently come and sit down by him, bring him pieces of coral, fine pearls, and . . . . shells . . . . Her presents were accompanied with smiles, pattings on the cheek, and all the marks of a most sincere and tender passion; but one day throwing her arms more than ordinarily eager about him, he began to be frightened that she had a design to draw him into the sea, and struggled till he disengaged himself, and then ran a good many paces from her; which behaviour she resented so highly . . . . that she took up a stone, and after throwing it at him, glided into her proper element, and was never seen on land again.   But the poor youth, tho' but slightly hit with the stone, felt from that moment so excessive a pain in his bowels, that the cry was never out of his mouth for seven days, at the end of which he died" (Waldron, *op. cit.*, pp. 131-2).   It seems probable that Collins in his foot-note is confusing Waldron's story of the mermaid and his traditional account of the magic mist which shrouded the island.   It is significant that the text harmonizes perfectly with Waldron's account of the mist. Possibly the footnote was added hurriedly just before publication and some time after the reading of Waldron and the writing of the ode, and that Collins's confused memory of Waldron, in whom he had found much to interest him, resulted in the curious "tradition", which also contains nothing at variance with Collins's lines, but of which there is, naturally, no other record.   Professor Kittredge, from his incomparably superior knowledge of writings relating to the Isle of Man, has kindly confirmed my opinion in this matter.

[62]*Lycidas*, l. 31.

istic of the poet's mind and can be paralleled in other poems.   Not a few of his best passages are tissues of literary reminiscence.   When he is drawing upon some more or less prosaic work for his basic materials, as in the case of Camden's *Britannia*, cited above,[63] he tends to *re-think* what he borrows into a more poetic language, not the conventional poetic diction of his day, but a language borrowed from Milton and his other favourites or minted from their dies; and in the process all sorts of vague and possibly little-recognized associations come into play.   Memory and her siren daughters had no small part in the creations of the disciple, as in those of the master—who spurned them. Within the inevitable limitations under which he works, Collins shows something of Milton's own power to combine and fuse and transfigure his materials by that inward power of thought and feeling which, for want of a better name, we call imagination, and whose workings we confess to be, in some sense, what Collins and the Wartons called them, *creative*.

Collins's imagination was, for all its vivid creations and its sudden and soaring flights, strangely lacking in sustained power, subject, it almost seems, to a sudden dereliction; and this is perhaps most apparent not when he is in quest of ideal beauty, at once vivid and subdued, but when, in the Pindaric odes, he is reaching out for an intenser experience of romantic passion, wonder and terror.   "This," says Johnson (to return to an omitted passage in his brilliant analysis), "was the character rather of his inclination than his genius;   the grandeur of wildness and the novelty of

---

[63]And even more strikingly in his borrowing from the writings of Martin Martin in the Superstitions ode, which falls outside the limits of this study.

extravagance were always desired by him, but not always attained." The critic has been anticipated in this judgment by the poet himself.

IV

What is the meaning of Collins's creative effort, taken in conjunction with Warton's critical protest, in the history of eighteenth-century poetry and in the early evolution of Romanticism? To answer that question we must glance at the prevailing tendencies of Neo-classical poetry, as we have already done at the prevailing tendencies of Neo-classical criticism. We must ask ourselves, what, in point of fact, is the place held by imagination in that poetry.

No one but the writers of text books now supposes that the Neo-classicists got rid of imagination by the simple process of repeating that reason was the superior power. The day is past of the unspoken argument: Dryden and Pope set reason above imagination; reason produces not poetry, but prose; therefore theirs was the *age of prose and reason*, and they themselves are *classics of our prose*. Indeed the wheel begins to come full circle when a popular critic pits Dryden's imagination against Milton's and Shelley's. Those whose homage to John Dryden will not carry them to these lengths, will, nevertheless, agree that there was in the masters of the Augustan age no radical deficiency in imaginative power. Wordsworth (in fairness be it remembered) conceded as much in the case of Pope, and Miss Sitwell has recently emphasized his rich endowment of imagination—at the expense of a number of other equally important truths. Yet it is obvious that the imagination in Dryden and Pope was directed to achievements radically different from either Milton's or Shelley's.

The peculiarity of the neo-classical imagination in England depends neither on defective vigour nor, in the last analysis, on undue conscious control (though this last has its importance); the peculiarity resides in the unsuual direction which the imagination takes. Instead of fastening, like the imagination of the Greeks and Shakespeare and Milton, upon some human experience, central, permanent, and universal in its appeal; instead of flying off, like the imagination of the great Romantics, to some land of heart's desire, of ideal beauty, pathos, or wonder, the imagination of Dryden and Pope, in their best and most typical writings, remained firmly anchored to the actual and the immediate. If their theory was predominantly classical, their practice was fundamentally realistic, albeit theirs was a selective realism. *Absalom and Achitophel*, to take only the best-known examples, is the greatest poem of its kind ever written, but it is inseparably tangled with the year 1681. Here is the central paradox of the Neo-classical period: a work whose general conception and whose detail bear the undeniable stamp of imagination, yet a work in which the imagination builds on, and to some extent with, hard prosaic facts. Or take *The Rape of the Lock*, where a fancy scarcely less exuberant than Shakespeare's rears its airy structure in the same way. *The Dunciad* is a classic which has perished in the morass of its own topical references; yet who can deny that even about these references an imagination, often unsavoury enough, plays, and who can withhold his admiration from its concluding flight?—

She comes! she comes! the sable throne behold
Of Night primaeval and of Chaos old!
Before her Fancy's gilded clouds decay,

And all its varying rainbows die away.
Wit shoots in vain its momentary fires:
The meteor drops and in a flash expires.
As one by one, at dread Medea's strain,
The sick'ning stars fade off th' ethereal plain;
As Argus' eyes by Hermes' wand opprest,
Clos'd one by one to everlasting rest;
Thus at her felt approach and secret might
Art after Art goes out, and all is night. . . . .
Religion blushing veils her sacred fires,
And unawares morality expires.
For public flame, nor private, dares to shine;
Nor human spark is left, nor glimpse divine!
Lo! thy dread empire, Chaos! is restor'd;
Light dies before thy uncreating word;
Thy hand, great Anarch! lets the curtain fall,
And universal darkness buries all.[1]

It may, of course, be argued that our examples are taken from satire and that satire always, in some degree, involves this adherence of the imagination to the actual and the immediate: Horace and Juvenal and Boileau do not escape the law. No doubt that is true; but it is only to say that wherever satire predominates it will prove that this peculiar direction of the imagination predominates—*as the cause.* From the very first Dryden had written not only for, but of, his little world, and except in translation he achieved but few successes beyond its limits; while Pope, once he was

---

[1] It is true that in the *Moral Essays* and the *Imitations of Horace* there is frequently less evidence of imagination than in the writings of Dryden or in the works of Pope cited, and it is, of course, precisely the *Moral Essays* and the *Satires and Epistles* to which Warton chiefly takes exception.

clear of "Fancy's maze," never paused in satirizing the life of his period save once, when he versified the philosophy of the coffee-houses for the coffee-houses. In this adherence to the actual and the immediate, Dryden and Pope are typical of the best creative literature of their period: the essays of Addison, in so far as they fall into this class, the comedies of Congreve, even the unpredictable effusions of Swift's genius betray, on or below the surface, the same limitation.[2]

Such a tendency as the one indicated above does not stop short with the selection of subject-matter: it informs the whole spirit in which the subject-matter is treated. The Neo-classical age in England exhibits a singular absence of the idealizing impulse: its realism extends from subject to thought and tone. It fails, for example, to rise to the conception of tragic heroism, the plane on which Sophocles and Shakespeare move; but it also escapes the sentimentality and pseudo-idealism of the next age. Its besetting weakness is cynicism. The Sentimental movement, which commences to develop early in the eighteenth century, is primarily a reaction against the cynicism of thought and letters in the Neo-classical period and its tendency to exalt the thinking head at the expense of the feeling heart. This movement synchronizes (not to penetrate here to their causal connections) with that growing demand which we have observed, for a freer and more creative imaginative activity. The first effects the liberation of the emotions; the second, that of the imagination. Together they make the middle decades of the eighteenth century the seed-

[2] Only Defoe stands half outside this generalization, and he pays his own peculiar tribute to the actual in his very manner of departing from it.

ground of the Romantic movement. Together they explain that tremendous interval in subject-matter, in outlook, and in tone, which separates such a poem as Shelley's *Prometheus* from Dryden's *Absalom and Achitophel*, or *The Ancient Mariner* from *The Rape of the Lock*.

The restricted action of the imagination in Neo-classical poetry corresponds, approximately at least, to the limited place assigned to that faculty in Neo-classical criticism. We have suggested that the predominance of the imagination was supposed to be incompatible with truth, and that nature, the criterion of truth, frequently tended to mean little more than empirical reality. Here is a further theoretical basis for the adherence of the Neo-classical imagination to the actual and the immediate.

The quest of truth in poetry had other results: it accounts in some measure for the didacticism with which Warton reproaches poetry in his day. The ethical is an important aspect of the true. Pope's boast makes clear this relation and also the supposed incompatibility of the imagination with truth and ethics:

That not in fancy's maze he wander'd long,
But stoop'd to truth and moraliz'd his song.

Didacticism is, of course, the monopoly of no period and no school: it is open to question whether Shelley, for example, or Tennyson is not often more offensively didactic than Dryden or even Pope, and it is certain that such Pre-Romantics as Thomson, Akenside, and Armstrong far outgo their predecessors in the pursuit of edification. Warton's diatribe against the didactic is, we have suggested, merely an aspect of his protest against the commonplace and the prosaic. He is thinking of those writings of Pope and his imitators, where the concepts of reason and the truths of morality are given pointed but somewhat unadorned expression. He dislikes the epigrammatic.[3] He is, apparently, not averse to preaching (having tried his own hand at it in *The Enthusiast*) so it be combined, as in the chief ethical-descriptive poets, with description, poetic ornament, and a certain imaginative expansiveness.

These poets, Thomson, Akenside, John Gilbert Cooper, and other contemporaries of Warton and Collins, inherit the neo-classical prepossession in favour of truth and nature in poetry and in favour of ethical reflection; but a different conception of nature and a different ethical creed[4] mark their writings off from those against which Warton inveighs.[5] The interest of the ethical-descriptive poets in nature extends from the universe as a whole to its parts. In its larger aspects this interest tends to break the adherence of the imagination to the actual and the immediate, and even in its lesser, to offer that faculty new material with which to work. The expansive spirit of their master Shaftesbury, slightly hazy and somewhat poetic, proved friendly to an imaginative type of moralizing, of which, indeed, he himself

[3] *Cf. Essay on Pope*, II, pp. 146-7. He himself consistently avoids it, as does Collins after the *Epistle to Hanmer*.

[4] The best analyses of both are by Mr. C. A. Moore, in his brilliant articles, *The Return to Nature in English Poetry* (*Studies in Philol.*, XIV, pp. 243 ff.) and *Shaftesbury and the Ethical Poets in England, 1700-60* (*P. M. L. A.*, XXI, pp. 264 ff.). See also *English Poets of the Eighteenth Century*, ed. E. Bernbaum, New York, 1918 (introduction) and W. E. Alderman's *Significance of Shaftesbury in English Speculation* (*P. M. L. A.*, XXXVIII, pp. 175 ff.).

[5] In the *Essay on Man* Pope is, of course, closer to these poets than elsewhere in his writings.

had given examples in prose. Warton, as revealed in *The Enthusiast*, is closer in his sympathies to this group than is Collins, and even in the odes he is less completely free from didacticism[6] than is his friend. It is Warton who makes the plea for *pure poetry*, but it is Collins who furnishes the consistent example of it. More than once it has been observed that he personifies the abstractions dear to the heart of the sentimentalist, Liberty, Simplicity, Pity; it has not been observed how singularly little he has to say about them. The rôle of his "persons" is imaginative and pictorial, not ethical, and on no subject, save his art, is he willing to advance a definite proposition in his poetry.

There is, however, a subtle connection between the demand for a freer and more creative activity of the imagination which Warton and Collins voice, and the Sentimental movement which the ethical-descriptive poets exemplify in a cruder form. It will be remembered that for Collins and Warton alike the *creative imagination* means a way to more varied and intenser experience. The power of feeling must be added to the power of conceiving:

Teach me but once like him to feel,[7]

Collins cries, referring to Shakespeare; and again, viewing the temple of Pity:

There let me oft, retir'd by day,
In dreams of passion melt away,
Allow'd with thee to dwell.[8]

[6]See, for example, the *Ode to Superstition*.
[7]*Ode to Fear*, l. 69.
[8]*Ode to Pity*, ll. 37-9.

As always, one must discriminate between Collins's desires and the extent to which they are achieved, between his inclination and his genius. That he desired intense emotional experience and that he sought it through the imagination admit of no doubt. The desire argues an attitude towards the emotions, fundamentally different from the reserved or even repressive attitude by which the peace of the Augustans was sought and in measure won.

It seems certain that the adherence of the Neo-classical imagination to the actual and the immediate, coupled with this reserved attitude towards the feelings, had contributed largely to the virtual obliteration of the lyric. Not until the death of Dryden does one witness the final sunset of seventeenth-century song; but the signs of decline have been long apparent. Among the various possible causes due weight should be given to two facts: that the best poetical talent was increasingly deflected to other types of verse more closely related to the life of the times, panegyric, satire, and argumentative poetry; and, what goes much deeper, that the quality of imagination and the tone and extent of feeling most common and most widely approved, were incompatible with a genuine and varied lyrism. The first forty years of the eighteenth century marks one of the most barren periods in the history of the lyric. It is ended by the advent of Collins and Gray. Their advent is accompanied by some severing of the imagination's bondage to the actual and is preceded by a more gradual but not less important series of changes in the sphere of the emotions.

During the Neo-classical era one type of lyric had abounded, the Pindaric ode. Johnson has made the right comment on the "pleasing fashion": "they that could do nothing else could write like Pindar." Despite the deplor-

able badness of most of the odes, they have a certain historical significance. When one has set aside those which
are merely panegyric verses disguised in irregular lines, and
has recognized that to some extent the music odes form a
class by themselves, there still remain a considerable
number, some on religious subjects, from which one can
deduce the Pindaric tradition, a tradition exercising some
influence even on the two classes isolated above. Poetic
enthusiasm, images beyond the realm of ordinary experience
and the strict rule of probability, a note of abandon—these
were among the conventions of the Pindaric:

> Wild as the lightning, various as the moon
> Roves my Pindaric song;

and its practitioners laboured hard to be both various and
wild, and to remember that, like Pindar, they must emulate
the mountain torrent. The Pindaric was hall-marked for
imaginative flights. The fact has a twofold interest: it
reveals the Pindaric as running in some degree counter to
the main current of poetry in the period, and it explains why
Collins turns naturally to this type of ode for his more
specifically romantic flights.

Something of the significance of Collins, with Joseph
Warton, in the history of eighteenth-century poetry and
in the early evolution of Romanticism should now be clear.
When all due reservations are made, it appears to lie in
their common insistence on the primacy of imagination in
poetry, in their conception of the imagination as a creative
power, and in the direction, in close harmony with their
theories, which Collins's imagination takes. By the
creative imagination they mean a power which can tran-

scend the limits of the actual and the immediate, and can create its own romantic world of freer and intenser experience.

This romantic world is to provide the subject-matter of poetry and to set its tone. In the *Odes* it is a world filled with bright visionary forms, symbolic of ideal beauty, pathos, wonder, and terror; but there is more beyond. Fairy shapes haunt its recesses; and old legends and the phrases of poets who have explored the realm before, echo through the stillness. The great Romantics will penetrate its depths and will not return empty-handed. But there is a fatality on those who would make this country their home.

A century after Collins, Charles Dickens remembered his early reading in the poet, and this is what he wrote:

"There was a fiction that Mr. Wopsle 'examined' the scholars once a quarter. What he did on these occasions was to turn up his cuffs, stick up his hair, and give us Mark Antony's oration over the body of Caesar. This was always followed by Collins's 'Ode on the Passions,' wherein I particularly venerated Mr. Wopsle as Revenge, throwing his blood-stained sword in thunder down, and taking the war-denouncing trumpet with a withering look. It was not with me then, as it was in later life, when I fell into the society of the Passions, and compared them with Collins and Wopsle, rather to the disadvantage of both gentlemen."[9]

Crude criticism, yet not without its truth! Collins was haunted by a sense of frustration; but the frustration which

[9] *Great Expectations*, chap. vii.

he feared is not the only one to which the Romantic poet is subject. There is the subtler danger that escaping from the actual he shall also lose his hold upon the real. Sometimes one is tempted to think of Collins as the first of the Romantics.

THE PANTISOCRACY SCHEME AND ITS IMMEDIATE BACKGROUND*

J. R. MacGillivray

THE wise and prudent have agreed from the first that Coleridge's scheme of forming a small equalitarian community on the American frontier, a pantisocracy as he named it whimsically, was an egregious absurdity, in the same class with projects for extracting sunlight from cucumbers and building houses by beginning at the roof, conceivable only in the Grand Academy of Lagado, or in the mind of Coleridge. Even Joseph Cottle, though a friend and patron of the Pantisocrats, almost immediately recognized the inanity of their plan, with a wisdom which he admits was quite beyond his years.

"Young as I was, I suspected there was an old and intractable leven in human nature, that would effectually frustrate these airy schemes of happiness which had been projected in every age, and always with the same result. At first the disclosure so confounded my understanding, that I almost fancied myself transported to some new state of things, while images of patriarchal and pristine felicity stood thick around, decked in the rain-bow's colours. A

*Note.—This account of pantisocracy requires some explanation, coming as it does, so soon after Sister Eugenia's article on the same general subject, which appeared in the *P.M.L.A.* for December, 1930. My excuse is three-fold. I have attempted to trace the background in a different way, concentrating especially on the significance of Brissot, Cooper, and Priestley, and their analogous schemes. I have had access to some evidence hitherto unused. Finally, a considerable part of this material was collected before the spring of 1930, and incorporated in an unpublished Harvard thesis.

moment's reflection, however, dissolved the unsubstantial vision, when I asked him[1] a few plain questions."[2]

But all his pertinent questions about ships, money, and similar practicalities, though couched most cunningly as by a kindly psychiatrist, failed completely to dispel the "epidemic delusion."

"It will excite merely an innocent smile in the reader, at the extravagance of a youthful and ardent mind, when he learns that Robert Lovell stated, with great seriousness, that, after the minutest calculation and inquiry among practical men, the demand on their labour would not exceed two hours a day; that is, for the production of absolute necessaries. The leisure still remaining, he said, might be devoted, in convenient fractions, to the extension of their domain. . . . . But after every claim that might be made on their manual labour had been discharged, a large portion of time, he said, would still remain for their own individual pursuits, so that they might read, converse, and even write books."[3]

And the reader has had his "innocent smile" at the naïve credulity of the Pantisocrats.

However, in recent years, and notably since the publication of Professor John Livingston Lowes' magnificent study, *The Road to Xanadu*, (surely a man and a book after Coleridge's own heart,) there has been rather less justification for a supercilious attitude toward the ill-starred

[1]Robert Lovell, who introduced Southey, Coleridge, and their plan to Cottle.
[2]J. Cottle, *Early Recollections*, I, p. 3.
[3]Ibid, pp. 8-9.

scheme of the Bristol enthusiasts. Another *pseudodoxia epidemica* of literary history has been called into question. For the Pantisocrats did not just blindly ignore practicalities. They did not conceive of their plan as an experiment to be conducted in a vacuum, a scheme isolated from the ordinary terms of life, and standing, to use Burke's famous phrase, in all the nakedness and solitude of metaphysical abstraction. They had sought out the most recent and authentic information about America. They had read books of travel, and had consulted with travellers in the flesh. They had inquired about land prices, bison, Indians, and mosquitoes. They had even made some preliminary financial calculations. In short, they had approached the scheme in what a business man,—and this is praise indeed —might have called a practical manner. Robert Lovell, at whose incorrigible illusions we have our innocent smile, did not learn of the two-hour working-day in Pennsylvania while communing with his own imagination, as Cottle implies. He found it, in all probability, in one of the most authoritative contemporary accounts of the country, *Nouveau Voyage dans les États-Unis de L'Amérique Septentrionale*[4] by J-P. Brissot, soon to be a distinguished statesman of revolutionary France and a leader of the party of the Gironde. Brissot himself had hoped to found a model republic in the American wilderness, and in 1788 had crossed the sea to spy out the new land of promise. Five years later an English liberal, Thomas Cooper, afterwards a professor in the University of Pennsylvania and later president of South Carolina College, visited America with a

[4]See below. A Harvard copy has the following inscription on the short-title page:—for the Library and University of Cambridge from the author. J. P. Brissot.

view toward establishing a similar place of refuge for the much-harassed radicals in his own land. He found the upper valley of the Susquehannah ideal for such a settlement, and announced it to all interested including the Bristol group, in *Some Information Respecting America*, his handbook for emigrant liberals. Finally, Dr. Priestley, one of the most distinguished scientists of his time, a Fellow of the Royal Society, not only went with his family to Pennsylvania expecting to join a colony of English emigrants there, but lived to the end of his days by the Susquehannah, near the place where the Pantisocrats had intended to settle, waiting in vain for the young English liberals who did not arrive. My purpose in this paper, then, is to outline the influence of Brissot, Cooper, and Priestley on pantisocracy, and to suggest that if Coleridge, Southey, and their fellows were deluded young men, they were such in the best company and with the best evidential justification.

The more remote background of pantisocracy needs concern us little. As Cottle informs us, "these airy schemes of happiness" have been "projected in every age." Indeed pantisocracy combines two traditions of human longing, the hope of an ideal commonwealth, and the nostalgic urge of sophisticated peoples toward the simple or primitive life, both of which are traceable back through the literatures of classical antiquity, and undoubtedly much further.

The cult of the primitive is as old as the story of Eden and the Song of Solomon. It is at the centre of the Taoist philosophy.[5] It can be followed through the pastoral

[5]Quotations may be taken almost at random from the sayings of

poetry of the Greek decadence, through Horace, (*vivitur parvo bene*) and the *Germania* of Tacitus. Mr. P. E. More tells us that the old idyllic dream is at the heart of even *Paradise Lost*,[6] and Tennyson would fain have it so. It is one of the most significant aspects of the romantic movement in the midst of which the pantisocrats lived.

As for the other tradition—Plato's ideal commonwealth,. as outlined in the later books of *The Republic* and in the fragmentary *Critias*, is the great prototype of many Utopian schemes. In the first century of our era Plutarch described the Spartan counterpart of Plato's commonwealth in his *Life of Lycurgas*. Two centuries later, Coleridge's master, Plotinus, planned to establish a platonic republic on the Campanian plains, but like the pantisocratic scheme it came to nought. Porphyry, in his life of Plotinus, tells us the story:—

"The emperor Gallienus and the empress Salonina, his wife, held Plotinos in high regard. Counting on their good will, he besought them to have a ruined town in Campania rebuilt, to give it with all its territory to him, that its inhabitants might be ruled by the laws of Plato. Plotinos intended to have it named Platonopolis, and to go and reside there with his disciples. This request would easily

---

Lao-Tzu to illustrate the point, *e.g.*

"Where the palaces are very splendid, there the fields will be very waste, and the granaries very empty. The wearing of gay embroidered robes, the carrying of sharp swords, fastidiousness in food and drink, superabundance of property and wealth:—this I call flaunting robbery; most assuredly it is not Tao."

    —*The Sayings of Lao-Tzu*, translated by Lionel Giles, *Wisdom of the East Series*, pp. 26-7.

[6]P. E. More, *Shelburne Essays, Fourth Series*, "The Theme of Paradise Lost."

have been granted but that some of the emperor's court!ers opposed this project, either from spite, jealousy, or other unworthy motive."[7]

So Platonopolis was not founded in Italy. In the following centuries the best thought in western civilization went toward the establishment of another commonwealth, the city of which Plotinus' greatest disciple wrote in his *De Civitate Dei*.

The discovery toward the end of the fifteenth century of new lands beyond the Atlantic provided Europe with an admirable locality for perfect commonwealths, imaginary and experimental. Here was a vast country, fruitful, sparsely populated, rich beyond man's imagining, and free to be occupied by any who had the courage to cross the sea. The land of heart's desire was within two months' sailing distance of Lisbon or Bristol—

> Earth's only Paradise
> Where Nature hath in store
> Fowle, Venison, and Fish,
> And the Fruitfull'st Soyle,
> Without your Toyle,
> Three Harvests more,
> All greater than you Wish.[8]

Moreover the new world was actually a new world. Here was a country whose inhabitants were entirely outside the pale of civilization,[9] unconfined by the *mores* of the tradi-

[7]Plotinus, *Complete Works*, (K. S. Guthrie's translation,) I, p. 19.

[8]Michael Drayton, *To the Virginian Voyage*.

[9]I leave the Aztec civilization out of account, but so too would an average Elizabethan.

tional cultures, even unaware, it would seem, of the original depravity of the human race and of the primal curse that by the sweat of his brow man must earn bread. The Americas were beautiful and the inhabitants thereof were idle. Surely the earthly paradise beyond the Pillars of Hercules had been rediscovered. Here was the place for men who would free themselves from the terms of life under Pope, Emperor and King. Hence to a great extent the revival of hope for an ideal commonwealth to be established somewhere beyond the confines of European civilization, a state which is variously imagined in More's *Utopia*, Bacon's *New Atlantis*, Campanella's *Civitas Solis* and Harrington's *Oceana*. Nor did the hope seem entirely vain. In New England there had been founded a commonwealth, theocratic in its government, modelled on the most perfect example which its founders could imagine, the ancient Israel which God himself had ruled; and if men were to judge by Cotton Mather's *Magnalia Christi Americana*, the history of the first eighty years of that theocracy, the experiment had proved to be as near a perfect success as could be expected in a world subject to sin. Writers of travel books, Bartram, Woolman, de Crèvecoeur, Imlay, Brissot, Cooper, seemed to rival one another in describing the beauty of the country and the virtue of its inhabitants, and in contrasting the felicity of the new world with the wretchedness of the old. "The task you have given me," wrote Gilbert Imlay at the beginning of his *Topographical Description of the Western Territory of North America*, "however difficult, I undertake with the greatest pleasure, as it will afford me an opportunity of contrasting the simple manners, and rational life of the Americans, in these back settlements, with the distorted and unnatural habits of the Europeans."

Obviously America was the place for those who would live simply and rationally. This became doubly certain after the triumphal conclusion of the revolutionary war. The Americans had won liberty by force of arms, and they were generous enough to welcome and strong enough to protect all who came to share their new freedom with them. America had been made safe for democracy, and,—who knows?—for pantisocracy too.

In the spring of 1788, a year before the meeting of the States-General, J.-P. Brissot, journalist and humanitarian, champion of Quakers, negroes, Americans, and mankind,[10] set out on his travels in the new world. M. Clavière, the Genevan banker, who had formed a company with two other financiers to speculate in the American national debt, provided Brissot with the money for his journey on condition that he would report on the financial condition of the country, and, strangely enough, on the possibility of forming an ideal state in the American hinterland. In a series of letters later incorporated in the *Nouveau Voyage*, Clavière issued final instructions to his emissary about to embark for America. I quote from Joel Barlow's English translation of 1792:—

LETTER III

"Plan of a Colony to be established in America.

May 21, 1788.

"When we contemplate the American Revolution, the circumstances which have opposed its perfection, the knowledge we are able to collect for the institution of re-

[10]See Brissot's *Examen critique des voyages dans l'Amérique septentrionale de M. le Marquis de Chastellux . . . . dans laquelle on réfute principalement ses opinions sur les Quakers, sur les Nègres, sur le peuple et sur l'homme. Londres*, 1786.

publics on a more perfect plan, the lands destined by Congress for new States, and the multitude of happy circumstances which may facilitate their preparatives, and protect their infancy, we are hurried insensibly into projects chimerical at the first sight, which become attracting by reflection, and which we abandon, but with regret, on account of the difficulty of finding a sufficient number of persons for their execution.

When a tract of land is offered for sale, and its limits ascertained, why cannot it be prepared, in all circumstances, for a republic, in the same manner as you prepare a house for your friends?"[11]

Be it remembered that this was no young poet who wrote, intoxicated by the strong wine of his own imagination, but a banker, forsooth, who not only proposed to establish a model state in America but expected to make a profit therefrom.   On the following page he continued:—

"I have no doubt, that, having acquired the soil, we might establish a republic, better calculated for peace and happiness, than any now existing, or that ever did exist. . . .

If men of wisdom and information should organize the plan of a society before it existed, and extend their foresight to every circumstance of preparing proper institutions for the forming of the morals public and private, and the encouragement of industry, ought they to be condemned as having formed a Eutopia? I do not believe it; it is my opinion, even that the love of gain, the love of novelty, and the spirit of philosophy, would lend a hand to an enterprise, which, before the American Revolution, might have been judged impracticable.

[11]*New Travels in the United States of America*, p. 59.

Profit, therefore, of your travels in America, to inform yourself, if, among the lands to be sold by Congress, there exists not a situation of easy access, where the nature of the soil is favourable to industry, and its other circumstances inviting to the first settlers."

On the next page one finds instructions which were followed exactly, though perhaps unwittingly, by the Bristol near-emigrants.

"After having acquired an exact idea of what may be expected from the nature of the soil, and its connection with neighbouring places, we might then undertake the work of forming a political and civil legislation, suited to the new republic, and its local circumstances. Such should be the task to be accomplished before the people departed from hence; that every settler might know beforehand what laws he is to live under, so that he will consent to them beforehand by choice."[12]

". . . . . These details will be sufficient to recall to your mind, our frequent conversations on a plan of this kind. If you can acquire from Congress the certainty of being able to realize it, so far as it depends on them, and we have only to find the company here to undertake it; I believe it may be easily done in Europe. . . . ."[13]

"It is useless to enter into more particular details on this matter; you know us: I shall only recommend to you an attention to the climate. A fine sky, temperature of Paris, no musketoes, agreeable situation, and good soil, are things indispensable."[14]

[12] pp. 62-3
[13] p. 64
[14] p. 70

These demands do seem rather high, but M. Clavière knew that he was sending his emissary to spy out the earthly paradise.

On June 3, 1788, Brissot sailed from Havre and on July 24th he disembarked at Boston.[15] Six days later he wrote to his patron, M. Clavière, describing the town, its people, and his own emotions.

"Boston, July 30, 1788.

"With what joy, my good friend, did I leap to this shore of liberty! I was weary of the sea; and the sight of trees, of towns, and even of men, gives a delicious refreshment to eyes fatigued with the desert of the ocean. I flew from despotism, and came at last to enjoy the spectacle of liberty, among a people, where nature, education, and habit had engraved the equality of rights, which every where else is treated as a chimera. With what pleasure did I contemplate this town, which first shook off the English yoke! . . . How I enjoyed the activity of the merchants, the artizans, and the sailors! It was not the noisy vortex of Paris; it was not the unquiet, eager mien of my countrymen; it was the simple, dignified air of men, who were conscious of liberty, and who see in all men their brothers and their equals. . . . . I thought myself in that Salentum, of which the lively pencil of Fenelon has left us so charming an image."[16]

In short Brissot thought that Boston and the inhabitants thereof were practically perfect, especially since they had ceased persecuting his friends the Quakers, and had abandoned most of their Puritan austerity. The same approval

[15]Eloise Ellery, *Brissot de Warville*, p. 71.
[16]J. P. Brissot, *op. cit.*, pp. 93-4.

was bestowed on Harvard University in spite of her unenlightened belief in the value of "the dead languages."

"The imagination could not fix on a place that could better unite all the conditions essential to a seat of education. . . .

"The buildings are large, numerous, and well distributed. . . . The library, and the cabinet of philosophy, do honour to the institution. The first contains 13,000 volumes. The heart of a Frenchman palpitates on finding the works of Racine, of Montesquieu, and the Encyclopaedia, where, 150 years ago, arose the smoke of the savage calumet."[17]

From July until December, 1788, Brissot remained in America, travelling, inquiring, taking copious notes of what he saw and heard. In general he was charmed by the new country, though he had his doubts about New York—"If there is a town on the American continent where the English luxury displays its follies, it is New York."[18] But for the smaller towns and the rural districts he had little but commendation. He was particularly delighted with what he heard of the country just beyond the Alleghenies, "An immense plain, intersected with hills of a gentle ascent, and watered every where with streams of all sizes; the soil is from three to seven feet deep, and of an astonishing fertility: it is proper to every kind of culture, and it multiplies cattle almost without the care of man."[19] Concerning central Pennsylvania where the Bristol emigrants later proposed to settle, Brissot received his information from two French

[17]pp. 106-7.
[18]pp. 156-7.
[19]p. 474.

naturalists, M. Saugrain and M. Piguet, who had recently returned from that happy country.

"The facility of producing grain, rearing cattle, making whisky, beer, and cyder, with a thousand other advantages, attract to this country great numbers of emigrants from other parts of America.   A man in that country, works scarcely two hours in a day, for the support of himself and family; he passes most of his time in idleness, hunting, or drinking."[20]

No wonder that the devoted band of pantisocrats decided that there was the country for them.   They would gladly work two hours a day; for some of the idleness, hunting, and drinking, they would substitute metaphysics, divine poesy, and the inspired Coleridge monologue, and who could ask more of life?

Brissot's plans for a settlement in America came to nought as far as he was directly concerned.   The impending revolution called him home from his travels, and before long he was too busy trying to establish a perfect commonwealth in France, to concern himself with the lands beyond the sea. Then came the multitudinous duties of office, the menace of the Jacobins, the struggle for survival, and finally in the autumn of 1793, the guillotine.   But his influence did not die with him.   In the spring of 1791 his *Nouveau Voyage* was published in Paris, and less than a year later an English translation in London.[21]   Both books seem to have had a considerable influence on emigration to America.   The French version became a source-book of information for the

[20]p. 260.
[21]The translator's preface is dated Feb. 1, 1792.

émigrés who found it discreet to put the ocean between themselves and the revolutionary tribunal, nor was the translation less useful to the English liberals who by 1794 had full cause to realize that the choice lay between freedom in America and compulsory emigration to Mr. Pitt's ideal colony for radicals at Botany Bay. As for the Bristol pantisocrats, we have certain evidence of their acquaintance with the *Nouveau Voyage*. Coleridge quotes directly from the translation, *New Travels in the United States of America*, in his own *Conciones ad Populum* delivered before the burgesses of Bristol in the spring of 1795.[22] In a letter to a friend of his, a clergyman, Tom Poole writes: "As for Brissot's book, I have read it in French; the translation has as much of the spirit and beauty of the original as a translation can possess. . . . . Happy had it been for France had all her leaders been like Brissot."[23] For several years Tom Poole had thought of emigrating to America himself, only to be restrained by business and family ties.[24] "I am weary of thinking of European politicks," he had written to his friend, Purkis, in June of 1793, "America seems the only asylum of peace and liberty—the only place where the dearest feelings of man are not insulted; in short, the only spot where a man the least humane and philosophical can live happily."[25] Or again in his letter of September 22, 1794, to Mr. Haskins who had inquired about pantisocracy, he writes:—"America is certainly a desirable country, so

[22]1795 version, pp. 31-32. I owe this lead to Professor Lowes:— *The Road to Xanadu*, p. 555.

[23]Mrs. H. Sandford, *Thomas Poole and his Friends*, I, pp. 112-3.

[24]See the letter of July 24, 1795, to his American friend, Mr. Garnett. Ibid, I, pp. 118-9.

[25]Ibid, I, pp. 77-8.

desirable in my eye that, were it not for some insuperable reasons, I would certainly settle there."[26] Brissot, too, seems to have had a strong personal influence on young Wordsworth, who although not a pantisocrat, was soon to belong to their circle. In another place I have pointed out evidence which would seem to show that Wordsworth lived in the same house with Brissot in Paris, and allied himself with his party and its aspirations.[27] Finally, Thomas Cooper, whose *Some Information Respecting America* was another text-book for the pantisocrats, not only had read the *Nouveau Voyage*,[28] but during his visit to France in the summer of 1792 had been personally acquainted in Paris with Brissot and his colleagues.[29]

Besides, there is a considerable amount of secondary evidence to show that the pantisocrats had carefully read, marked, and inwardly digested the contents of the *Nouveau Voyage*. Lovell's contention that they would have to work only two hours a day in central Pennsylvania seems to have been taken directly from the glowing report of that country by M. Saugrain and M. Piguet, quoted above. Their whole method of procedure in planning their commonwealth looks remarkably like the one outlined by M. Clavière for his emissary, Brissot. Their naïve faith that they could establish a colony of their own, enact their own laws and regulations, and having bought the land which they would occupy, could hold it as sovereign possessors without inter-

[26]Ibid, I, pp. 98-9.

[27]*Times Literary Supplement*, Jan. 29, 1931.

[28]Cooper quotes both Brissot's *New Travels* and Imlay's *Account of the New American Settlement of Kentucky* in his own *Some Information Respecting America*, p. 23. See below.

[29]See below: note 35.

ference from federal or state authorities, seems to have been the belief, at least at first, of M. Clavière and probably of Brissot too. One more possible point of contact may be noted. In the translator's preface to *New Travels in the United States of America* there is a footnote recommending Jedediah Morse's *American Geography* as the best source of information about the new republic. Now since the publication of *The Road to Xanadu* we have known one important thing about Coleridge's reading habits, that he not only read footnotes, but that he frequently, in fact habitually, read works there quoted or recommended. It is perhaps significant, then, that one finds in the *American Geography*, 1789, the information that Northumberland county on the west branch of the Susquehannah is only one-tenth occupied by settlers, and the additional note that"a very large proportion of the vacant lands in the state are in this county, (Northumberland County, Pennsylvania,) to the amount of about eight millions of acres."[30]. The pantisocrats seem to have read their Brissot carefully.

From the account of Brissot and his probable influence on pantisocracy we turn to Thomas Cooper, the author of *Some Information Respecting America*. Cooper was born at Westminster in 1759.[31] At the age of nineteen he matriculated at University College, Oxford, but he failed to take a degree, possibly because he refused to subscribe to the Thirty-Nine Articles. During his whole life his religious opinions seem to have been decidedly unorthodox. A

[30]*The American Geography*, Elizabethtown, 1789, p. 303.

[31]For an account of his life see Dumas Malone, *The Public Life of Thomas Cooper*, Yale University Press, 1926, or H. M. Ellis, "Thomas Cooper—A Survey of his Life," *South Atlantic Quarterly*, XIX, pp. 24-42.

historian of the University of South Carolina, of which Cooper became president, wrote less than twenty years ago: "Men are still found in South Carolina who have heard from their fathers and they from their fathers, that Thomas Cooper was an atheist and that his spirit still hovers over the University."[32] Nor was his conduct, any more than his religious views, conformable to propriety. His father wanted him to study law, and entered him at the Inner Temple, but the wayward son decided otherwise, determined to become a physician, attended anatomical lectures, studied chemistry, and joined a company of calico-printers at Bolton, near Manchester. Nor were his political opinions any better. He soon became a friend and disciple of Dr. Joseph Priestley, a political and theological radical. As early as March 7, 1787, we hear of him reading his *Propositions respecting the Foundation of Civil Government* before the Literary and Philosophical Society of Manchester.[33] He was an early advocate of the abolition of slavery. Charles James Fox, writing on January 11, 1788, to Thomas Walker, the chairman of the Manchester committee for the abolition of slavery, remarks in postscript:—

"Upon looking over my letter I find I have forgotten taking notice of what you say of your intention of making me acquainted with Mr. Cooper. I shall be very happy to be acquainted with a gentleman who has taken so spirited a part in this business (abolition), and whose love of liberty seems to be so genuine and sincere."[34]

[32] Edwin L. Green, *A History of the University of South Carolina*, Columbus, S.C., 1916, p. 36.

[33] Thomas Cooper, *A Reply to Mr. Burke's Invective*, pp. 78-88, where the speech is reprinted. It had been published previously in the transactions of the society, 1790, Vol. 3, p. 481.

[34] Thomas Walker, *The Original*, I, p. 108.

On the outbreak of the French Revolution, Cooper became a radical with the best of them, an exceedingly active member of the Manchester Constitutional Society, and in the spring of 1792, along with James Watt, a son of the inventor, the bearer of fraternal greetings from the Manchester society to the Jacobin Club in Paris. Unfortunately there is no room here for an account of that interesting and graceless escapade, by which these two English Jacobins won general notoriety and the magnificent denunciations of the great Edmund Burke himself. Suffice it for our purpose to say that in Paris Thomas Cooper was on intimate terms with the Brissotins.[35] Perhaps it was through Brissot's influence that the National Assembly conferred French citizenship on Cooper, as well as on his friend Priestley and others.[36] Certainly after his return to England in the summer of 1792, Cooper considered himself on friendly terms with Brissot. When Captain Imlay, the husband of Mary Wollstonecraft and an agent for lands in Kentucky, arrived in Paris, "probably about February, 1793," he carried a letter of introduction from Cooper to

[35]See *Cyclopaedia of American Literature* (E. A. and G. L. Duyckinck, ed.), II, p. 332. *Memoranda of Table Talk of Judge Cooper*. "I kept company principally with the Brissotians (sic). . . . . One evening, at the house of a person whose name I did not catch, where many Brissotians were present, Watt and I proposed that if they would gather as many friends as they could and go with us, to support us at the (Jacobin) club, I would insult Robespierre before the whole assembly, and compel him to challenge us to fight. We should have broken him up that night. . . . . but d—m the bit these fellows would agree to join us."

[36]The *Patriote* for Sept. 25, 1792, announced that French citizenship had been conferred on Thomas Cooper, John Horne Tooke, Thomas Christie, and Joel Barlow. W. Godwin, *Memoirs of Mary Wollstonecraft*, (W. C. Durant, ed.,), p. 224, note. Priestley and Paine had been granted the same honours the previous August 26th.

Brissot.[37] In the Public Record Office there is a provocative postscript to one of Captain George Munro's secret despatches from Paris to the British Foreign Office: (December 21, 1792) "A person from Manchester has arrived this day from that place, and brings Letters from Mr. Cooper, I dont yet know his name but shall find it out before Mondays post."[38] Unfortunately Munro did not find it out, or if he did, he forgot to tell Lord Grenville about it. It is just possible that the date of Imlay's arrival in Paris is given six weeks too late by the editor of Godwin's *Memoirs*, cited above, and that the unknown newcomer with his letter from Cooper was Imlay himself.

The next summer, while Brissot was imprisoned in Paris and within two months of his execution, Cooper determined to make an exploratory visit to America for himself, with a view to verifying the possibility of establishing a free settlement in the western lands which Congress was selling. Two of Joseph Priestley's sons accompanied him. On July 24, 1793, Dr. Priestley wrote from Wooton to his friend, the Reverend Theophilus Lindsey:

"I leave this place Friday, having heard that Joseph will be the next day at Clapton, ready to embark with Mr. Cooper from London, in about a fortnight."[39]

On August 5 he wrote from Clapton as follows:

"I am now, however, a great deal occupied about the departure of my sons for America. Mr. Cooper goes with

[37]W. Godwin, *op. cit.*, p. 262.
[38]F.O. 27. 40.
[39]J. T. Rutt, *Life and Correspondence of Joseph Priestley*, II, p. 204

them, and Mr. Walker[40], who has not yet left London, will follow."[41]

On August 24, Cooper himself wrote Samuel Rogers from Deal, just before he sailed to America.[42]

Cooper spent the autumn and winter of 1793 in America, and sailed again from New York for England, with sheaves of notes on the new country, in February, 1794.[43]   In the spring the notes were set in order, and then published by Joseph Johnson of St. Paul's Churchyard, as *Some Information Respecting America.*   Under the large map at the front of the book, the date of publication was given as "Augt 12th. 1794."

Cooper weighed carefully the merits of various districts and by a process of elimination decided unequivocally in favour of the upper valleys of the Susquehannah as the ideal place for a settlement.   "I prefer," he writes, "in a general view, Pennsylvania to New York."   A little further on he confines his preference still further:—

"Moreover, the largest unoccupied tracts of land, of course the cheapest, and beyond comparison the richest lands in this state, are to be found in the northern parts of the counties just mentioned, (Northumberland, Luzerne, and Northampton) and of Allegany county; that is, generally speaking, north of latitude 41°.   Of these I prefer the eastern, rather than the western division, because a vicinity to the branches of the Susquehanna, which will convey produce to Philadelphia and Baltimore, is and ever will be

[40]The Manchester radical mentioned above.
[41]J. T. Rutt, op. cit., II, p. 205.
[42]P. W. Clayden, *Early Life of Samuel Rogers*, p. 285.
[43]Thomas Cooper, *Some Information Respecting America*, preface.

much more valuable, than the neighbourhood of those waters that communicate at present only with the Ohio."[44]

In another place he writes:—

"It is evident from hence (as indeed it is from a simple inspection of the map) that the interior parts of Pennsylvania, in the vicinity of the Susquehannah, where the land for the most part is extremely fine, have very considerable advantages over the most advantageous part of the Genesee tract, in the facility of transporting produce to market."[45]

And again:

"You will wonder perhaps that I have said so little about the *Shenandoah Valley*, which Brissot has recommended; or of *Kentucky*, that land of promise, of which Imlay has given so flattering a description."[46]

And from that text he elaborates again on the superior merits of the Susquehannah country. In another letter he continues:

"You ask me, what sum is necessary to commence farmer (*sic*) upon a moderate scale, in some civilized, and tolerably well settled part of the back country?

"A man may buy 300 acres of rich, but unimproved land, for instance, at present in such a situation, for 30s. per acre, currency, payable by instalments. . . .

"You ask me why I prefer the place* I mentioned to you for settling?   Because, first . . . ."

[44]p. 19.
[45]p. 13.
[46]p. 23.

and so on for another page. The asterisk indicates an interesting footnote:

"*This relates to a proposed settlement in Pennsylvania on the Loyalsock creek; and extending between the east and the west branches of the Susquehanna, about 40 or 50 miles from Sunbury, and about 170 from Philadelphia."[47]

It was a definite, practical, earthy scheme of Cooper's, upon which Coleridge and the pantisocrats built.' They did not choose the valley of the Susquehannah for the sake of the romantic name,[48] but because it was recommended by the best informed authorities, and because the friends of liberty were already forming a settlement there.

For meanwhile, before the publication of Cooper's book, and evidently several months before Coleridge or Southey had heard of the Susquehannah, the first devoted emigrants had abandoned England for those happier lands. Cooper had left part of his family in America, so he soon returned.[49] Dr. Priestley, two of whose sons were already there, welcoming a chance to leave a country where his house had been burned and his scientific manuscripts destroyed by Church and King hoodlums,[50] took Cooper's advice and emigrated with his wife and family to the land of refuge. In the British Museum there is an interesting letter written by Priestley to Lord Auckland about three weeks before he left: (Add. Mss. 34, 543 f. 392.)

[47]p. 73. See also the part of Cooper's map, showing the Susquehannah country, opposite page.

[48]As Coleridge whimsically told Dr. Gillman in later years. James Gillman, *Life of S. T. Coleridge*, p. 69.

[49]*Some Information Respecting America*, preface.

[50]In July, 1791. See Joseph Priestley, *Memoirs*, I, p. 118; *An Appeal to the Public*, etc., pp. 1-43.

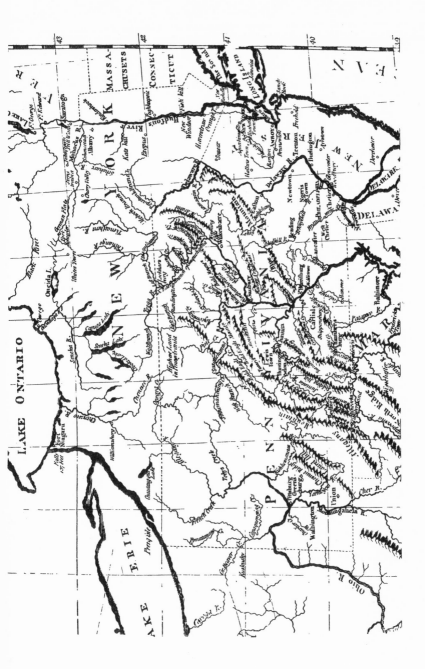

"My Lord

"Having occasion to apply to some person near the seat of power, I have no hesitation from a former acquaintance, and my real esteem for your Lordship, to have recourse to you.

"Being about to leave this country I am desirous of doing it with as much security as I can: and as the ship in which I go is an American (The Sansom Capt. Smith for New York) liable to capture by the Algerians, I am desirous of getting a protection (?) from their government. A young man, who lately went to Philadelphia told me that he had procured one, promising it (*sic*) to return it unopened if it should not be wanted, and I am ready to promise the same.

"If your Lordship can procure me this favour, I shall remember it with gratitude tho I may have no opportunity of thanking you in person.

"With much respect, I am,
           "My Lord,
                "Your Lordships
                    most obedient humble Serv
                                        J. Priestley"
Clapton, March 21, 1794
   "P.S. I go with my wife, a maid servant and a boy. We expect to sail on Monday next."

Dr. Priestley's expectations were not exactly fulfilled for his ship was delayed. The curious may examine *Lloyd's List* and learn that the *Sansom*, Captain Smith, sailed from Gravesend on April 7, and from Deal on the 10th, bound for New York.

In his *Memoirs*, composed about two years after, Dr. Priestley outlined his relations to the Susquehannah scheme.

"At the time of my leaving England my son in conjunction with Mr. Cooper, and other English emigrants, had a scheme for a large settlement for the friends of liberty in general near the head of the Susquehanna in Pennsylvania. And taking it for granted that it would be carried into effect, after landing at New-York, I went to Philadelphia, and thence came to Northumberland, a town the nearest to the proposed settlement, thinking to reside there until some progress had been made in it. The settlement was given up; but being here, and my wife and myself liking the place, I have determined to take up my residence here, though subject to many disadvantages."[51]

And at Northumberland, at the forks of the Susquehannah, Priestley lived until his death in February, 1804, waiting in vain for the "other English emigrants." There he was joined by Thomas Cooper and his family,[52] and there they set up a common scientific laboratory toward the advancement of knowledge in the American wilderness. But "the friends of liberty" did not come.

Meanwhile, failing English emigrants to the Susquehannah country, Priestley and Cooper seem to have tried to encourage settlers from France, of which country they

[51]p. 126-7. There are several pages on the proposed Susquehannah colony written by Joseph Priestley, Jr., in the same *Memoirs*, p. 165 ff.

[52]Evidently Cooper remained in England for a short time after Priestley's departure. He had come back to England to help defend his friend Thomas Walker, who was in prison awaiting trial for "Conspiracy to overthrow the Constitution and Government, and to Aid and Assist the French (being the King's Enemies), in case they should invade this Kingdom." Walker was tried at Lancaster in the first week of April, and acquitted. T. B. Howell, *State Trials*, XXIII, p. 1055.

had been elected honorary citizens.[53]   In the Bibliothèque
Nationale there is a pamphlet entitled:—*Plan de Vente de
Trois Cent Mille Acres de Terres Situées dans les Comptés de
Northumberland et de Huntingdon dans l'État de Pensylvanie,
. . . . à* Philadelphia, 1794." At the bottom of the title
page there is written: "Par M[r]. Cooper pour sa Compagnie
avec le Dr. Priestley."[54] While "the friends of liberty" in
Bristol were trying in vain to secure the necessary capital
for their enterprise, the Susquehannah country was being
put up for auction by Dr. Priestley and Thomas Cooper.[55]
La Rouchefoucauld-Liancourt, who in May, 1795, in the
course of his American travels, visited Northumberland and
its distinguished citizens, Priestley and Cooper, has given
us an account of his experiences in his *Voyage dans les
États-Unis d'Amérique.* He found Northumberland "dans

[53]See note 36 above.

[54]See M. W. Kelley, "Thomas Cooper and Pantisocracy." *Mod.
Lang. Notes,* April 1930, pp. 218-20. This pamphlet had been noticed
previously several times. See Bernard Faÿ, *The Revolutionary Spirit
in France and America,* p. 317. Also Bernard Faÿ, *Bibliographie
critique des ouvrages française relatifs aux États-Unis* (1770-1800), p. 32.

[55]In the *Gentleman's Magazine* for June, 1795, p. 515, there appears
this paragraph:

AMERICAN NEWS

"There is a Colony established not far from the Susquehannah River,
in America, by a class of wealthy Frenchmen, who formerly distinguished
themselves in the Constituent Assembly of France, but were prudent
enough to retire in time with their families and property; among
these are Noailles, Talon, Blaçon, Talleyrand, and others of the
ci-devant Noblesse; they have relinquished their titles, and have
domesticated here in the most social manner. Their little settlement
is called Frenchtown. The Tavern is kept by an officer, who was
formerly le Baron Beaulieu!" Frenchtown is in Delaware, near the
mouth of the Susquehannah. See Morse's *Universal Geography,* 1796,
I, opposite p. 566.

une des plus belles situations que l'on puisse rencontrer."[56]
However, the village itself was hardly in keeping with its
situation. "C'est sans doute une des plus mal bâties que
nous ayons vue encore. Maisons de bois, la plupart log-
houses, deux seulement, dans la totalité, sont bâties en
briques et en pierres; point de marché, quatre ou cinq
mauvaises tavernes à whiskey; nous sommes dans le
meilleure, et il pleut sur nos lits, comme dans l'écurie où
sont nos chevaux."[57] A different picture, this, of the
Susquehannah country, from the accounts which the
pantisocrats had read in the works of Brissot and Cooper.
Of the proposed settlement at the forks of the Susquehannah
and its failure, La Rochefoucauld-Liancourt also writes:

"Son fils,[58] arrivé quelque tems avant lui en Amérique,
lui avait acheté des terres où devaient venir se réunir, sous
l'étendart du docteur, tous les Unitairiens et tous les
persécutés d'Angleterre. Cet établissement devait recevoir
protection et honneur du gouvernement Américain, et créer
au docteur une existence de fondateur de colonie, et de
chef de secte.

"Toutes ces illusions se sont bientôt évanouies: les
Anglais ne sont point arrivés pour acheter ses terres, et le
gouvernement des États-Unis, celui même de Pensylvanie,
n'ont pas considéré le project d'établissement du docteur,
plus que celui de tout autre."[59]

[56]*Voyage dans les États-Unis d'Amérique, fait en 1795, 1796 et 1797.*
Par La Rochefoucault-Liancourt. . . . . à Paris, ... L'An VII de la
République, I, p. 121.

[57]Ibid, I, p. 122.

[58]Dr. Priestley's son, who had accompanied Cooper to America in the
late summer of 1793.

[59]*Op. cit.,* I, pp. 129-30.

And now leaving Dr. Priestley to his disillusionment, let us turn to one group of "les Anglais qui ne sont pas arrivés," and trace in outline the rise, decline and fall of the Bristol pantisocracy.

The general scheme, whereby a little model state was to be established somewhere in America, based on equality of rank and community of property, seems to have been well under way before Cooper's book was published in London in August, 1794. Probably the idea originated with Southey.[60] In a letter to Horace Bedford on November 13, 1793, and in another to Grosvenor Bedford on the following December 14, he was imagining a utopia in America.[61] But it was not until the following spring that emigration was seriously considered. Early in June of that year, at the beginning of the Long Vacation, Coleridge (sometime Private Silas Tomkyn Comberbacke of the 15th Light Dragoons and new released from a month of incarceration with the works of Demetrius Phalareus) left Cambridge to pay a visit at Oxford. Supposedly, he was on his way back to his home at Ottery St. Mary in Devon. At Oxford he fell in with Southey, and the two of them were soon deep in pantisocracy.[62]. The Oxford visit lasted about a month; and at the end of that time, on Saturday morning, July 5,[63]

[60]C. C. Southey thought that not his father, but Coleridge, originated the scheme: *Life and Correspondence of R. Southey*, I, p. 211.

[61]*Ibid.*, I, pp. 193-6.

[62]By June 12, Southey wrote to Grosvenor Bedford: "Allen is with us daily and his friend from Cambridge, Coleridge. . . . ." *Life and Corr. of Southey*, I, p. 210.

[63]The chronology of the Welsh tour can be determined. In a letter of July 22nd (*Biog. Ep.*, I, p. 35), Coleridge gives the route and stars the places where they slept. Gloucester was the first night's stop from Oxford; and he was at Gloucester on July 6 in the morning. (*Letters*, I,

Coleridge started off with his friend Hucks, not home to Devon, but on a walking tour in Wales. One may estimate the strength of his enthusiasm from the letter which he wrote back to Southey the next morning from Gloucester, after a walk of fifty odd miles from Oxford.[64]

". . . . When the pure system of pantisocracy shall have *aspheterized*—from ά, non, and σφέτερος, proprius (we really *wanted* such a word), instead of travelling along the circuitous, dusty, beaten highroad of diction, you thus cut across the soft, green, pathless field of novelty! Similes for ever! Hurrah! I have bought a little blank book, and a portable ink horn; (and) as I journey onward, I ever and anon pluck the wild flowers of poesy. . . . .

"Farewell, sturdy Republican! Write me concerning Burnett and thyself, and concerning etc., etc. My next shall be a more sober and chastened epistle. . . . To Lovell, fraternity and civic remembrances! Hucks' compliments."[65]

At Llanfyllin, he told Southey in a letter ten days later, "I preached pantisocracy and aspheterism with so much success that two great huge fellows of butcher-like appearance danced about the room in enthusiastic agitation.[66]

And at the end of the letter:

"I have positively done nothing but dream of the system of no property every step of the way since I left you, till last Sunday. Heigho!"

p. 73) Ergo,— The itinerary is given with dates, also at the end of Hucks', *A Pedestrian Tour*, pp. 157-160.

[64]Forty-seven miles by Hucks' estimate: *op. cit.*, p. 157.
[65]*Letters* (E. H. Coleridge, ed.), I, pp. 73-4.
[66]*Letters*, I, p. 79.

At Bala his zeal was still rising. In fact he nearly caught the itch from fraternity with "a Welsh democrat," and something else from four good Tories before whom he proposed the health of Dr. Priestley, the pre-pantisocrat who was just establishing himself by the Susquehannah.[67]

And so the summer passed. On Sunday, August 3rd, after trudging six hundred miles up hill and down dale, preaching pantisocracy and aspheterism to all comers, Coleridge and Hucks arrived in Bristol to rejoin their fellow-citizens of the new commonwealth.[68] On August 18th, while on their way to hold a council with George Burnett down in Somersetshire, Coleridge and Southey first met Tom Poole of Nether Stowey. Fortunately he took the two of them over to see his nephew, John Poole, who happened to be keeping a diary. His description, translated from the original school-boy Latin of the diary, runs as follows:—

"Rise about eight. After breakfast go to Mr. Lewis's and get the loan of Boswell's *Life of Johnson* from him. About one o'clock, Thomas Poole and his brother Richard, Henry Poole, and two young men, friends of his, come in. These two strangers, I understand, had left Cambridge, and had walked nearly all through Wales. One is an undergraduate of Oxford, the other of Cambridge. Each of them was shamefully hot with Democratic rage as regards politics, and both Infidel as to religion. I was extremely indignant. At last, however, about two o'clock, they all go away.

[67] *Biographia Epistolaris*, I, pp. 36-7.

[68] See J. Huck's, *op. cit..* Huck's last letter is addressed from "The Old Passage" on August 2. In the list of towns through which they passed, given in the appendix, we learn that they reached Bristol the next day.

After dinner I betake myself to the *Life of Johnson*. About seven o'clock, Mr. Reekes comes from Stowey; he is very indignant over the odious and detestable ill-feeling of those two young men, whom he had met at my Uncle Thomas's. They seem to have shown their sentiments more plainly there than with us. But enough of such matters. . . . ."[69]

Whether with all this pedestrian touring, this shocking of church-folk and outraging of Tories, it ever occurred to Coleridge to go the thirty miles further to see his mother at Ottery St. Mary is open to question. It seems unlikely unless for only a day or two, because he was "nearly five weeks" at Bristol and Bath, and in London by the first week of September.[70] Pantisocracy was too important to permit one to waste time in mere visiting.

[69]Mrs. H. Sandford. *Thomas Poole and his Friends*, I, pp. 103-4. It is probably significant that three days after Tom Poole received these two young heretics in his home, "a very particular friend" of his informed him that he "was considered by the Government as the most dangerous person in the county of Somerset." Ibid, I, p. 92.

[70]On Sept. 6, Coleridge wrote to Southey what was evidently the first letter after their separation. *Biographia Epistolaris*, I, p. 42. This letter was from London. When he arrived at Cambridge on Sept. 17 and wrote to Sarah Fricker, a fortnight had elapsed since his departure from Bath. *Letters*, I, p. 85. This evidence fits perfectly with Southey's "nearly five weeks." In a letter of Sept. 20, 1794, to his sailor brother, Tom, Southey wrote:—"Coleridge was with us nearly five weeks, and made good use of his time. We preached Pantisocracy and Aspheterism everywhere. These, Tom, are two new words, the first signifying the equal government of all, and the other the generalization of individual property; words well understood in the city of Bristol. We are busy in getting our plan and principles ready to distribute privately. . . . . The thoughts of the day, and the visions of the night, all centre in America. Time lags heavily along till March, but we have done wonders since you left us." C. C. Southey, *Life and Corr. of R. Southey*, I, p. 221.

In London Coleridge lost no time to advance the cause. On September 6 he wrote to Southey:—

"The day after my arrival I finished the first act:[71] I transcribed it.   The next morning Franklin (of Pembroke Coll. Cam., a *ci-devant Grecian* of our school—so we call the first boys) called on me, and persuaded me to go with him and breakfast with Dyer, author of *The Complaints of the Poor, a Subscription*, etc. etc.[72] I went; explained our system. He was enraptured; pronounced it impregnable. He is intimate with Dr. Priestley, and doubts not that the Doctor will join us. . . . . Every night I meet a most intelligent young man, who spent the last five years of his life in America, and is lately come from thence as an agent to sell land.   He was at our school.   I had been kind to him; he remembers it, and comes regularly every evening to "benefit by conversation," he says.   He says £2000 will do; that he doubts not we can contract for our passage under £400; that we shall buy the land a great deal cheaper when we arrive in America than we could do in England; "or why," he adds, "am I sent over here?"   That twelve men may *easily* clear 300 acres in four or five months; and that, for 600 dollars, a thousand acres may be cleared and houses built on them.   He recommends the Susquehanna for its excessive beauty and its security from hostile Indians. . . . .   He never saw a *bison* in his life. . . . . The mosquitoes are not

[71]Of *The Fall of Robespierre*.   It was through the press three weeks later. *Letters*, I, p. 87.

[72]George Dyer had been a student at Christ's Hospital, hence possibly his interest in Franklin and Coleridge.   In the letter of Sept. 19, Coleridge writes:—"In London . . . . I was taken ill, very ill. I exhausted my finances, and ill as I was, I sat down and scrawled a few guineas's worth of nonsense for the booksellers, which Dyer disposed of for me." *Letters*, I, p. 84.

so bad as our gnats; and, after you have been there a little while they don't trouble you much."[73]

Say what one will about the pantisocracy scheme, one strange and unexpected fact keeps emerging, that it was Coleridge more than any of the others—except perhaps Mrs. Fricker—who kept his two feet on solid reality. It was he who sought out the opinion of the experts, who read the books of travel, consulted with persons who knew the country, counted the cost, learned about land values, Indians and mosquitoes, and was generally the practical man of the party. To be sure, he had his illusions. He had no very clear notion of where the prerequisite two thousand pounds was to be obtained. He lacked a saving awareness of the intractable old Adam in man—until he saw its workings in his fellow-citizen, Southey. But withal he had a restless energy which they lacked, a persistent faith in the scheme, and a desire to learn everything that was to be known. He read Cooper's *Some Information Respecting America* carefully. "What think you," he wrote to Southey on October 21st, "of the difference in the prices of land as stated by Cowper (*sic*) from those given by the American agents? By all means read, ponder on Cowper, and when I hear your thoughts I will give you the result of my own."[74]

Undoubtedly there was a connection between the pantisocracy scheme and the settlement for English friends of liberty planned by Priestley and Cooper between the east and west branches of the Susquehannah, but its exact nature and extent is difficult to determine from the available evidence. Undoubtedly Coleridge learned the details of

[73]*Biographia Epistolaris*, I, pp. 42-3.
[74]*Letters*, I, pp. 91-2.

Priestley's plan from George Dyer by the first week of September. He probably first read Cooper's *Some Information Respecting America* at the same time. Dyer gave him reason to believe that the great Dr. Priestley himself would become a pantisocrat. But whether Priestley ever heard of such a thing is entirely another matter. His own plans were rather different. As La Rochefoucauld-Liancourt tells us, his son had bought large tracts of land at the forks of the Susquehannah "ou devaient venir se réunir, sous l'étendart du docteur, tous les Unitairiens et tous les persécutés d'Angleterre. Cet établissement devait. . . . . créer au docteur une existence de fondateur de colonie, et de chef de secte." Now at this time both Coleridge and Southey, like Dyer, Priestley and Cooper were Unitarians, and sufficiently persecuted to be eligible for membership in Priestley's colony. But whether they could ever have combined "the pure system of pantisocracy" with Priestley's plan for a Unitarian colony of which he would be patriarch, is a difficult question. The journey was abandoned before there was that bridge to cross.

On September 17, Coleridge returned to Cambridge from London, to preach pantisocracy at the University. At ten o'clock the next morning he was writing to Southey:

"Well, my dear Southey! I am at last arrived at Jesus. My God! how tumultuous are the movements of my heart. Since I quitted this room what and how important events have been evolved! America! Southey! Miss Fricker! Yes, Southey, you are right. Even Love is the creature of strong motive.[75] I certainly love her. . . . .

[75]The "strong motive" was pantisocracy. Southey had been insisting that it was Coleridge's duty to fall in love with Sarah Fricker, who was to be a pantisocrat, and to give up his hopeless devotion to

"Pantisocracy! Oh, I shall have such a scheme of it! My head, my heart, are all alive. I have drawn up my arguments in battle array; they shall have the *tactician* excellence of the mathematician with the enthusiasm of the poet.

"Brookes and Berdmore,[76] as I suspected, have spread my opinions in mangled forms at Cambridge. Caldwell, the most pantisocratic of aristocrats, has been laughing at me. Up I arose, terrible in reasoning. He fled from me, because "he could not answer for his own sanity, sitting so near a madman of genius."[77]

It is not surprising that after an autumn when pantisocracy was everything, Coleridge gave up all thought of obtaining his degree.

Meanwhile the scheme was being enlarged to include others beside Coleridge, Southey, Lovell, Allen, and their immediate friends from Oxford and Cambridge. Favell, still at Christ's Hospital, had joined. The Fricker sisters from Bath were to go, Edith as Mrs. Southey, Mary as Mrs. Lovell, Sarah as Mrs. Coleridge, Martha in splendid isolation in spite of George Burnett, and even Mrs. Fricker herself, recalcitrant though she was, as the mother-in-law of pantisocracy. Southey's mother, too, was to be included.

Mary Evans. Southey won. This determination of his, however, to marry all the Fricker sisters to pantisocrats, received a rude shock when Martha refused George Burnett's proposal. One suspects, perhaps unkindly, that Mrs. Fricker bore with pantisocracy only as long as it provided suitable matches for her numerous daughters.

[76]Fellow Cantabs, whom Coleridge and Hucks had met at Aberconway on a pedestrian tour in a post-chaise, had laughed at "famously," and joined for a few days. *Biographia Epistolaris*, I, pp. 37, 40.

[77]*Letters*, I, pp. 81–2.

Further, a few select persons, still more remotely connected, were invited to join the colony. Early in the autumn[78] Coleridge wrote to Charles Heath, an apothecary at Monmouth, as follows:

"Sir,

"Your brother has introduced my name to you; I shall therefore offer no apology for this letter. A small but liberalized party have formed a scheme of emigration on the principles of an abolition of individual property. Of their political creed, and the arguments by which they support and elucidate it they are preparing a few copies— not as meaning to publish them, but for private distribution. . . . . With regard to pecuniary matters it is found necessary, if twelve men with their families emigrate on this system, that £2000 should be the aggregate of their contributions—but infer not from hence that each man's *quota* is to be settled with the littleness of mathematical accuracy. No; all will strain every nerve; and then, I trust, the surplus money of some will supply the deficiencies of others. The *minutiae* of topographical information we are daily endeavouring to acquire; at present our plan is, to settle at a distance, but at a convenient distance, from Cooper's Town[79] on the banks of the Susquehanna. This,

[78]The large number of common factors to be found in this letter, in Southey's of Sept. 20, 1794 (note 71, above), and in Coleridge's of Sept. 6, quoted above, would suggest some time in September for the date.

[79]"Cooper's Town, Pennsylvania, is situated on the Susquehannah river. This place, in 1785, was a wilderness. Nine years after, it contained 1800 inhabitants; a large and handsome church, with a steeple . . . . a library of 1200 volumes, and an academy of 64 scholars." —Morse's *American Gazetteer*, 1797.

however, will be the object of future investigation. For the time of emigration we have fixed on next March. In the course of the winter those of us whose bodies, from habits of sedentary study or academic indolence, have not acquired their full tone and strength, intend to learn the theory and practice of agriculture and carpentry, according as situation and circumstances make one or the other convenient.

"Your fellow Citizen,
"S. T. Coleridge"[80]

On September 15th still another applicant, Josiah Haskins of Honiton, Devon, wrote to Tom Poole to inquire about the scheme. I quote from the letter now in the British Museum.[81]

"Sidmouth 15th Septem^r. 1794

".... Your Brother whom I the other day saw at Sherborne informs me of a scheme which some Friends of yours are about putting into execution,—that of a migration into America— As this is an Idea which I have long entertained, I should be much gratified in being favoured with the particulars respecting it—whether (as it seems it is in the plan of forming a new Colony) the number of Emigrators are limited or not—what their Qualification—what the Ideas in which they proceed (are) like.

"If you will in as short a time as you conveniently can, give me information with respect to this, you will do me great service.

"Could you make it convenient at any time, I should be *particularly* happy to see you at Honiton.

[80]*Biographia Epistolaris*, I, pp. 44-5.
[81]Add. Mss. 35, 344 f. 219.

"Excuse this short letter and believe me,
            "Dear Sir,
                        "Yours most sincerely
(Address)   "Jos[h]. Haskins."
W. Haskins
Sidmouth, Devon

Tom Poole's long and informative reply to this letter is printed at length in his biography.[82]

But already by the middle of September, when new recruits were being enlisted each week from the market-towns of the west country, and when Coleridge was waging victorious war with scoffers at Cambridge, it became clear that all was not entirely well with pantisocracy. Two days after his arrival in Cambridge, Coleridge received a harsh letter from Southey, rebuking him for not writing more often to Sarah Fricker, whom he must court and marry for the sake of pantisocracy.[83] The letter was soon forgiven, but hardly forgotten. But other difficulties soon appeared. There were the children, for example. Men and women carefully chosen, disciplined to obey reason, might make successful citizens of the millennial commonwealth. Children born in the new world could be educated from the cradle in the principles of pantisocracy and aspheterism. But what of the others, little Frickers and Southeys, at the brat stage and incorrigible? "These children,—the little Frickers, for instance, and your brothers,"—Coleridge wrote to Southey, "are they not already deeply tinged with the prejudices and errors of society? Have they not

[82]Mrs. H. Sandford, *Thomas Poole and his Friends*, I, pp. 96-9. This letter is the best single statement of the scheme, but too long to be quoted at length, and too closely written to be broken.

[83]*Letters*, I, pp. 84-6.

learned from their schoolfellows *Fear* and *Selfishness*, of which the necessary offsprings are Deceit and desultory Hatred?"[84] They could hardly be left behind, yet if taken along they would be "subversive of *rational* hopes of a permanent system."

Then Southey fell from grace with his outrageous demand that they must take servants with them to do the hard work. They, the apostles of equality, to introduce servantage into their society! "My feeble and exhausted heart regards with a criminal indifference the introduction of servitude into our society," wrote Coleridge in despair, "but my judgment is not asleep, nor can I suffer your reason, Southey, to be entangled in the web which your feelings have woven."[85] And so pantisocracy fell gradually into decay. Soon Burnett, Lovell, and Southey were arguing in favour of buying a common farm in Wales, and abandoning the original scheme entirely. "Your private resources were to remain your individual property," wrote Coleridge a year later, "and everything to be separate except a farm of five or six acres. In short, we were to commence partners in a petty farming trade. This was the mouse of which the mountain Pantisocracy was at last safely delivered."[86] By December 11, 1794, Lovell was writing to Thomas Holcroft, asking his and William Godwin's blessing on the proposed farm in Wales.[87] Coleridge found himself alone, the only one of them who was willing to attempt the original project.

[84]*Letters*, I, p. 102.

[85]*Letters*, I, p. 95. Also pp. 101-2.

[86]*Letters*, I, p. 140. It is part of Coleridge's long indictment of Southey's conduct, in the letter of Nov. 13, 1795.

[87]*The Life of Thomas Holcroft written by himself*, etc. London. 1925, II, pp. 83-4.

"Southey! Pantisocracy is not the question," wrote Coleridge in October, 1795, "its realization is distant—perhaps a miraculous millennium. . . . ."[88] The desired millennium did not come. The Welsh plan died as wretchedly as its American predecessor. Soon Southey was exploring Portugal instead of Pennsylvania, and Coleridge was campaigning in the Midlands for *The Watchman*. Meanwhile, Joseph Priestley and Thomas Cooper waited in vain by the Susquehannah for the English emigrants who did not come.

[88]*Letters*, I, p. 134.

SHELLEY'S RELATION TO BERKELEY AND DRUMMOND

G. S. Brett

I.

IN the year 1922 a century had elapsed since the death
of Shelley. The occasion stimulated the lovers of
poetry and, more particularly, the friends of Shelley to
review and reconsider their estimate of Shelley's life and
work. Under the same influence I turned my attention
again to the familiar pages. They had been read almost
in childhood, and to the child their value had consisted in
musical rhythms and emotional power. But at this later
period, with other interests and ideas, a new attraction
was offered by the subtle forms of expression and the
curious exactness of the phrases. This led to new considerations about the actual meaning of the words and so to a
theory which is embodied in this essay. Its object, in
brief, is to restate in an improved form the view that
Shelley was guided in the formation of his ideas by a
scientific and philosophical standpoint to a degree which
has not hitherto been fully realized.

For this statement, if it seems too bold or paradoxical, I
would offer a defence and an explanation. Poetry has
both form and matter. It presents infinite variety in
both respects, and attracts different minds by very distinct
qualities. The poet may choose to produce different effects
at different times: his aim is sometimes pure music,
sometimes direct vision of reality, sometimes mystical or
symbolic suggestion of a reality which he does not wholly
embody in his words. When some or all of these aims

are combined, the critic is liable to dismember the living creation and hold up to view one or other of the detached aspects as the only or the most important organ in the body of the poet's work. Shelley certainly impresses himself upon the reader as primarily inspired, exuberant, and ecstatic. He was described by Matthew Arnold as "a beautiful and ineffectual angel, beating in the void his luminous wings in vain." He was told, by no less a person than Keats, that he must curb his exuberance and try to be more of a poet. These and similar traditional phrases have guided generations of readers, who have felt thereby justified in yielding themselves to the buoyant rapture of Shelley's language and allowing the ferment of his strong imagination to cloud their own intellects. This view of Shelley is easy and pleasant: its popularity is thereby explained. But if Shelley returned to-day I believe he would declare it false and assert that it was not vague feeling but clear understanding that gave wings to his words. Before he could attain spiritual freedom and express the fullness of his nature Shelley had to find salvation in a new philosophy. My first undertaking is to show that this philosophy was a genuine metaphysical standpoint, that it was not merely a vague echo of Platonic phraseology, and that it alone explains many favourite modes of expression consciously employed by Shelley to set forth this particular theory.

The evidence at this point is of the highest quality. In Shelley's works, edited by H. Buxton Forman, Vol. VI, we have the fragmentary essay *On Life*, one of a group of similar essays in which Shelley is seen formulating the significance of his general philosophical attitude. The note prefixed to this essay quotes the following explanation as given by Mrs. Shelley:—

"Shelley was a disciple of the immaterial philosophy of Berkeley. This theory gave unity and grandeur to his ideas, while it opened a wide field for his imagination. The creation, such as it was perceived by his mind—a unit in immensity, was slight and narrow compared with the interminable forms of thought that might exist beyond, to be perceived perhaps hereafter by his own mind: or which are perceptible to other minds that fill the universe, not of space in the material sense, but of infinity in the immaterial one."

In the essay itself there are one or two very striking statements which I will quote as I consider them decisive for the whole interpretation of Shelley's views.

"The view of life presented by the most refined deductions of the intellectual philosophy is that of unity. Nothing exists but as it is perceived. The difference is merely nominal between those two classes of thought, which are vulgarly distinguished by the names of ideas and external objects. Pursuing the same thread of reasoning, the existence of distinct individual minds, similar to that which is employed in now questioning its own nature, is likewise found to be a delusion. The words I, you, they, are not signs of any actual difference subsisting between the assemblage of thoughts thus indicated, but are merely marks employed to denote the different modifications of the one mind."

In an earlier passage of this essay Shelley says:—

"The most refined abstractions of logic conduct to a view of life, which, though startling to the apprehension, is, in fact, that which the habitual sense of its repeated combinations has extinguished in us. It strips, as it were, the painted curtain from this scene of things. I confess that I am one of those who am[1] unable to refuse my assent to the conclusions of those philosophers who assert that nothing exists but as it is perceived."

This is a very explicit statement and leaves no room for doubt as to Shelley's adoption of this philosophy. It will be useful here to draw attention to a point in Shelley's method of expressing himself. Here he says that the philosophy "strips as it were the painted curtain from the scene of things": in the Adonais this is transposed and stated so as to explain the origin of the painted curtain; this is done in the well-known lines:

> Life like a dome of many-coloured glass
> Stains the white radiance of eternity.

But before any attempt can be made to study the evolution of Shelley's typical phrases it is advisable to make a statement of the exact doctrine to which Shelley gives the name "immaterialism." This requires unusual care and watchfulness. Shelley is a disciple but not an imitator: his obvious ignorance of what is usually acquired in the routine of academic work is counterbalanced by freshness and originality: his mind broods over a phrase or idea until it is shaped and transformed into the likeness of his intuition. On account of these peculiarities Shelley's thoughts and words never prove quite true to type: the seed is genuine but the fruit is unexpected: we set out with the conviction that we are to have one more version of Platonism, or one more variation on the well-worn theme of Prometheus; but

[1]This is the usual grammar of the Romantic School!

unless we remain blinded by this conviction, we shall soon find that in fact we are not keeping to any beaten track.

The immaterial philosophy of Berkeley was not strictly platonic: it was nearer to some forms of neoplatonism and has indeed a somewhat indefinite relation to the whole history of idealism. Berkeley made the great discovery that all problems of knowledge must begin from the question—How does experience become objective? The ancient problem of vision was thus solved. In place of the innumerable theories invented to explain the transmission of something from a distant object through a medium into the eye and thence into the mind, Berkeley proposed to take as a primary fact the experience we have in vision and show how this becomes a system of signs capable of being translated into the externality of the world of space and motion. The idea was very simple and it was in fact ready to hand in a long tradition which begins from Plotinus in the third century. But it was often misunderstood, and easily ridiculed. To the artist it is obvious, because distance for him is perspective: he knows the language of vision and, so to speak, writes his descriptions in it; a simple rule of proportions suffices for him when he wishes, in the common language, "to put one thing behind another." But the success of the artist is due to the fact that he employs the actual stuff of our experience: the distant object looks smaller than the near object, and as a matter of experience, therefore, this difference of proportions is the essence of distance as we perceive it. For it is clear, on reflection, that experiences cannot be either nearer or further: they are all equally where the self is.

The first objection foolishly brought against this simple analysis of experience is expressed by the assertion that it reduces things to ideas and finally makes all the world simply the contents of my mind. So Samuel Johnson, who could be at times excessively and stupidly practical, thought he refuted the idealistic philosophy by kicking at a stone in the road. The theory actually changed nothing except the errors of ordinary judgments: it was no *more* revolutionary than the discovery that the image in a mirror is not another person: and we may add that it was also no *less* revolutionary. Shelley understood the real meaning of this "immaterialism" and estimated it properly, for he makes the following very important comment:—

"Philosophy, impatient as it may be to build, has much work yet remaining as pioneer for the overgrowth of ages. It makes one step toward this object: it destroys error and the roots of error. . . . . It reduces the mind to that freedom in which it would have acted, but for the misuse of words and signs, the instruments of its own creation. By signs, I would be understood in a wide sense, including what is properly meant by that term, and what I peculiarly mean. In this latter sense, almost all familiar objects are signs, standing not for themselves, but for others, in their capacity of suggesting one thought which shall lead to a train of thoughts. Our whole life is thus an education of error."

It is clear that this philosophy produced upon Shelley a peculiar and deep effect. It seems to have solved for him some baffling problem. He did not proceed to build upon it any formal philosophy, either critical or constructive, but accepted it as the essence of his thought and the atmosphere of his life. As a poet he desired primarily to feel and to express. Henceforth he was free to satisfy the cravings of his nature, because the great obstacle had been removed. What was that obstacle? The answer to this question is crucial and must be carefully considered. I think the answer must be found in the way Shelley regarded *persons*. The material philosophy hampered him because it gave him only a world of bodies and made him look on all persons as individuals rigidly separate and mechanically impenetrable.[1] With the discovery of the immaterial philosophy this terrible separateness of persons vanished: there was no more any necessity to think of persons as primarily flesh and blood; on the contrary the form, the voice, the look are our own experiences, the sense-material through which the other person is revealed; and that other person in its inner self is what we are, a living experience. If, then, two persons have the same thoughts, the same feelings, are they not truly one? In the language of mech-

---

[1]The following passage from Drummond, *Academical Questions* Bk. i, ch. vi, pp. 61-2, seems to be the justification of this view:—"A German philosopher, who was a better calculator than a metaphysician, has asserted that impenetrability must be an essential property of matter, because two bodies cannot occupy the same space at the same time. But to this the idealist may answer, that the inference is not necessary, because the case may be differently stated, and the difficulty otherwise solved. We are not, he may say, perceptive of bodies, but of those images which are immediately present to our minds. If it be said that matter is impenetrable, because two bodies cannot be at once in the same place, the reason given must presuppose the fact. Now this is precisely what the sceptic calls in question. He seems also to explain the difficulty more satisfactorily when he says, that we cannot confound, or blend into one, two distinct and separate ideas, than the materialist, who first imagines two prototypes of those ideas, and then accounts for the impossibility of their filling something likewise imagined, which he calls *space*, at the same *time*, which is also something determined, as it is perceived and understood, by attributing to those prototypes a quality, the existence of which I have shown he cannot prove."

anical philosophy, with its time and space and matter, they cannot be: but that world is now transcended: it is not the only reality: it has no more ultimate value than the ink and paper which similarly embody the meaning of a poem.

In this way Shelley grasps the idea that the immaterial philosophy makes possible the unity of all things. This is shown very clearly in the quotation above, where we are told that the existence of distinct individual minds is a delusion. This passage also shows how Shelley limited his discovery in philosophy to the one question of personality: this was his dominant interest, and his almost morbid sense of isolation doubtless contributed much to his use of the "intellectual" philosophy.

The theory of Berkeley does not necessarily involve the conclusion that the universe is simply a diffused mind or reason. Even if this was a legitimate conclusion it was not that which Shelley adopted. He was content with the less extravagant view that matter is the vehicle of spirit and that spirit always needs some vehicle such as the structure of a plant or the organism of the animal body. Shelley is so little inclined to give independent reality to thought in the manner of extreme mystics, that he conjectures it may be no more than a relation. In his essay *On a Future State* he says:—"It is probable that what we call thought is not an actual being, but no more than the relation between certain parts of that infinitely varied mass, of which the rest of the universe is composed and which ceases to exist so soon as those parts change their position with regard to each other. Thus colour and sound and taste and odour exist only relatively."

In view of such passages as these we must avoid the hasty conclusion that Shelley was a pantheist or an advocate of

Universal Reason in the sense in which mystical idealism uses those terms. What we actually find in Shelley is the belief that all particular things are ways in which certain elementary particles combine. The "infinitely varied mass" is thus capable of becoming all things and all things may again be resolved into it. What this mass actually is, Shelley, I think, nowhere states, but it may be correct to say that he actually thought of it as a plastic force for which the nearest analogue would be a material substance like fire. This might seem to contradict the whole doctrine of "immaterialism" by finally making the substance of the universe a kind of matter. But the point is irrelevant and due to misunderstanding. The doctrine of Berkeley only asserted that particular things take on the form of the mind that perceives them: the mind like a prism creates for itself a world of colours and then fails to realise the pure light which it has thus split up into a seeming variety. But "the many pass and change" while the One abides. It is this One which we are now seeking to define. The common view seems to be that Shelley meant by the One what the mystics of all ages mean by Cosmic Reason. On the contrary he must have meant something which was not personal at all but was the substance from which persons are evolved as the colours from pure light. The suggestion which I wish to make is that in fact all this part of Shelley's language is due to his acquaintance with another and less known part of Berkeley's work, the essay on tar-water.

Whether the Bishop of Cloyne was or was not in earnest when he advocated tar-water as a medicine need not be discussed. His method of popularizing the drug was to write a work called *Siris: A Chain of Philosophical Reflexions & Inquiries concerning the Virtues of Tar Water*. This is, in fact, a very learned and genial description of what has been said by Greeks, Romans, Egyptians, Chinese and others on the nature of soul, body, and fire. The topics are not irrelevant, for health is very much a question of soul and body, while the supreme virtue of tar-water consists in the fact that it embodies fire. We are told that "the luminous spirit lodged and detained in the native balsam of pines and firs is of a nature so mild and benign, and proportioned to the human constitution, as to warm without heating, to cheer but not inebriate."

In this last phrase we have a link between Berkeley and the poets: very few of those who quote Cowper's line— "The cup that cheers but not inebriates"—could find it in Berkeley's works. Perhaps, if we could know the whole truth, Berkeley's *Siris* was the source of many other ideas which seem to depend on profound erudition. Unfortunately the work is so diffuse that only a feeble idea of its character and contents can be given here, and it will be necessary to select for mention the points which seem significant in the present context. After the first 136 paragraphs devoted to records of the qualities and effects of tar-water, we are introduced to the general chemical theory, namely, that "salt, water, oil and earth seem to be originally the same in all vegetables," and "all the difference ariseth from a spirit residing in the oil," called by the chemists the native spirits. This leads to a lengthy excursus on the air, "the receptacle as well as source of all sublunary forms." There is some "latent vivifying spirit dispersed throughout the air," and men are agreed that it must be "the same thing that supports the vital and the common flame." Air, then, is really an aggregate of the volatile parts of all natural beings, which "become air by acquiring an elasticity and volatility from the attraction of some active subtle substance whether it be called fire, aether, light, or the vital spirit of the world."

At this point Berkeley makes a transition to the next link in his chain—the discussion of this aether or pure invisible fire, "the most subtle and elastic of all bodies," which "seems to pervade and expand itself throughout the whole universe." "This mighty agent," says Berkeley, "is everywhere at hand, ready to break forth into action, if not restrained and governed with the greatest wisdom. Being always restless and in motion, it actuates and enlivens the whole visible mass, is equally fitted to produce and destroy, distinguishes the various stages of nature, and keeps up the perpetual round of generations and corruptions, pregnant with forms which it constantly sends forth and resorbs. So quick in its motions, so subtle and penetrating in its nature, so extensive in its effects, it seemeth no other than the Vegetative Soul or Vital Spirit of the World."

This theme is, of course, not at all new and Berkeley duly refers to Pythagoreans, Platonists and Stoics as having held that there is an animal soul in man, the instrumental and physical cause of sense and motion. Mind or spirit is the only real cause: to speak of corporeal "causes" is to use the term in an improper sense. Mind or soul always requires a medium or instrument whereby to act, and this is fire. Soul acts on fire, and fire acts on air. Ethereal fire or light comprehends in a mixed state "the seeds, natural causes, and forms of all sublunary things": these are separated out by attraction and repulsion, so that individual things appear in much the same way that a prism evolves distinct colours from pure light. Berkeley, true to his original bent in philosophy, was prepared to make the theory of vision a basis for the explanation of all things. This extension of the theory of light is so far peculiar and important that it is excusable to quote a passage which sums up the whole doctrine:—

"Blue, red, yellow, and other colours have been discovered by Sir Isaac Newton to depend on the parted rays or particles of light. And, in like manner, a particular odour or flavour seemeth to depend on peculiar particles of light or fire: as appears from heats being necessary to all vegetation whatsoever and from the extreme minuteness or volatility of those vegetable souls or forms, flying off from the subjects without any sensible diminution of their weight. These particles, blended in one common ocean, should seem to conceal the distinct forms, but, parted and attracted by proper subjects, disclose or produce them. As the particles of light, which, when separated, form distinct colours, being blended are lost in one uniform appearance."

Further on we are told that "In the Timaeus of Plato there is supposed something like a net of fire and rays of fire in a human body. Does not this seem to mean the animal spirit flowing, or rather darting, through the nerves?"

Next in order comes a long and learned discourse concerning Plato, the Egyptians, and many others who had written on light, terminating with the evidence of the Psalmist, who also had said: "Thou art clothed with light as with a garment." Diverging again into scientific detail, Berkeley discusses questions of attraction and repulsion: he rejects purely mechanical laws of action as only secondary and refers all real causality to more occult agents and affinities. He quotes with favour the view that "the hidden force which unites, adjusts and causeth all things to hang together and move in harmony" is intelligent Love. "This Divine Love and Intellect are not themselves obvious to our view, or otherwise discerned than in their effects. Intellect enlightens, Love connects, and the Sovereign Good attracts all things." The *Siris* concludes then with a comprehensive survey of all the important parts of the usual Platonic tradition, such as the permanence of reality, the ceaseless flow of things sensible and perishing, the supremacy of Reason as akin to the Divine Nature. It is not necessary to give any account of this revived Platonism since our object is not to deal with what is common to all Platonists but with such peculiarities or variations as seem to make Berkeley a distinctive source of inspiration to Shelley.

II

Reference was made above to the evolution of Shelley's typical phrases. This was not an incidental remark but the statement of a fact which, if it can be established, must be considered very important for the student of Shelley's ideas. It means, in brief, that we can trace the history of some central ideas quite clearly; and also that Shelley went through an elaborate process of formulating the idea in the phrase which satisfied his standard of poetic diction.

The proof of this consists in showing first the importance of a remark, made by Mrs. Shelley, that Shelley was led to his philosophical position by reading Sir William Drummond's *Academical Questions*. In view of this statement I took the obvious step of acquiring the book and considering what it offered. Drummond was probably born in 1770 and, more certainly, died in 1828. He was a scholar and diplomatist: he became a Fellow of the Royal Society in

1799. But he was like others of his day in uniting with other pursuits a rather amateurish liking for current philosophical speculations and a cultured appreciation of literature. He first attracted attention in 1795 by a work entitled *A Review of the Governments of Sparta and Athens*. In 1798 he published a translation of the *Satires of Persius*. In 1817 he wrote an original poem called *Odin*, of which only Part I was published. In 1824 he began to publish *Origines or Remarks on the origin of several Empires, States, and Cities*. Four volumes were finally produced, the last in 1829. Another work was entitled *Oedipus Judaicus*, described as a commentary on parts of Genesis, Joshua, Judges, etc.[1] Obviously Sir William had wide and varied interests. *The Academical Questions* was published in 1805. The copy which I consulted in 1926 was in the library of Harvard University and was dated 1816. The contents are well indicated by the title. "Academical" seems to mean philosophical or speculative, and the "questions" are general problems of metaphysics, science and morals. The present use of this volume is limited to the passages which seem to be related to Shelley's ideas and phrases.

It is essential to the present thesis to recognize that no theory can be accurately called Platonic if it rests on the doctrine that white light is physically compound and can be analysed into the colours of the prismatic scale. This is not Platonic but Newtonian, and, while there may be a sense in which Shelley was a Platonist (certainly an admirer of the *Symposium*), the prominence of the Newtonian view should temper the language of the essayists, who revel in

---

[1]See *Dictionary of National Biography* for other data. The account here given is not complete.

their use of the word Platonic for everything that is unusual or philosophical.

In the first part of this essay it has been shown that Shelley acquired a view called the immaterial philosophy. This was derived from Berkeley, who made his reputation by writing a theory of vision, and in his more general philosophy expanded the Newtonian theory of light to support the view that all individual forms *may* be contained in the Primal Unity, the apparent plurality of life being a kind of refractive (Newtonian) separation. This, we now assert, is one of Shelley's dominant ideas. But it is further to be shown that it came to him through the medium of Sir William Drummond's book. Since we have the evidence that Shelley read the book, it only remains to discover what it may have offered him.

To appreciate the relationship between Drummond and Shelley it is necessary to know the leisurely way in which Drummond handles his themes. The *Questions* is not a systematic work: it is a book of glimpses into attractive realms of thought, decorated with no small display of learning, reminiscent of everyone from Pythagoras to Kant, akin in spirit and style to Berkeley. The so-called English empirical philosophy takes the place of honour, but Sir William clearly writes as an unprofessional philosopher, who will only swallow what science and common sense can digest. Here we are compelled to present him abstractly in a few selections, with such comments as may justify the procedure.

(1) Acad. Quest. Bk i, Ch. ii, p. 25
"When we desire to analyse what any thing is, which we denominate an external object, we always find that it may

be resolved into certain sensible qualities. If I be desired to explain what I perceive when I examine a fine marble statue, I can only repeat the catalogue of my own feelings. I say that I am sensible of the whiteness of the stone, of the beauty of the form, and of the justness of the proportions; that I feel hardness, and smoothness; and that I judge differently of its magnitude, while I observe that magnitude under different visual angles. Thus then, instead of describing the external statue, I am in fact expressing my own sentiments, stating my own feelings, declaring my own judgments, and detailing perceptions which exist only in my own mind.

"The active and passive states of external objects are determined by changes, which take place in their sensible qualities. But what are these qualities of external objects, unless they be sensations in our own minds, which we have attributed to things supposed to exist around us? We cannot define, nor describe, what we neither feel nor perceive. Nothing can be felt, nor perceived, where it is not. The changes, which exist in our own feelings, and in our own perceptions, must be erroneously stated to have had place in remote and exterior objects."

.   .   .   .

This passage states clearly the method of analysis which was used by Berkeley and which leads to the "intellectual philosophy" adopted by Shelley. The word "erroneously" seems to suggest a source for Shelley's rather curious phrase "Our whole life is thus an education of error" (*i.e.* we learn that we had begun by erroneously taking the inner to be outer).

(2) Acad. Quest. Bk. i, Ch. iv, p. 45.

"The author of philosophical arrangements, who could only gain a glimpse of the primary matter by abstraction, obtains a sight of it by analogy. *We obtain a sight of it,* he observes, *when we say, that as is the brass to the statue, the marble to the pillar, the timber to the ship, or any one secondary matter to any one peculiar form, so is the first and original matter to all forms in general.*

"There is no word in the language of the Peripatetics more difficult to be understood than *form.* Sometimes the soul is itself a form; sometimes it is the place of forms. It is form, which makes body obvious to sense; yet the first form is not cognizable by the senses. Nothing can be distinguished unless it be under some particular form. There is, nevertheless, a general form, abstracted from all individual things, which is universal with respect to all beings. Form may be differently considered as substance and as accident, since the Peripatetics seem not quite decided, whether it be the one, or the other. It exists rather in power than in action; and may be either eductive or receptive. We are then to obtain a sight of the primary matter by saying, that it is to universal form what secondary matter is to peculiar form."

Acad. Quest. Bk. i, Ch. iv, p. 41.

"*We gain a glimpse of it by abstraction,* observes the learned author of philosophical arrangements, *when we say that the first matter is not the lineaments and complexion, which make the beautiful face; nor yet the flesh and blood, which make those lineaments, and that complexion; nor yet the liquid and solid aliments, which make that flesh and blood; nor yet the simple bodies of earth and water, which make those various aliments; but something which, being below all these, and supporting them all, is yet different from them all, and essential to their existence."*

These passages are specimens of Drummond's discussion of forms. He seems to be uncertain what "form" means: probably, like most eighteenth century writers, he was not sure of the difference between Aristotle and Bacon. He decides that we can assert a First Being, which is "primary matter," but none-the-less is not "matter," but rather "force." This rather loose exposition, which it is useless to emend, is very much like the version of Greek philosophy provided by the Scotch professors of the period. It is necessary to remember that serious study of historical philosophy did not begin till the time of E. Zeller; in other words after Hegel (d. 1831). For this reason it is useless to argue about texts: what is called Plato may often be Cudworth or Henry More, and what is called Aristotle may be anything at all. But Drummond does at least grasp the point that the creative power is *natura naturans* (he often quotes "Spinoza") and not Jehovah.

Shelley, we may suppose, found this quite congenial. It is noteworthy that Drummond goes out of his way to emphasize Parmenides. (*Acad. Quest.* Bk. ii, Ch. iv, p. 243.) He objects to the interpretations which "Platonize," and agrees with Cudworth that the "one *ens*" of Parmenides is a "principle superior to mind": it is in fact a neutral substance from which both mind and matter take their origin. We may suppose that the "esemplastic" principle of Coleridge is to be defined in the same way and that Shelley manipulates this concept when he writes:

While the *one Spirit's plastic* stress
Sweeps through the dull dense world, compelling there
All new successions to the *forms* they wear.

As we have argued above (p. 187), this is not the Creator
of the Hebrews but the creative power of the 'physical'
Greek philosophers."

(3) Acad. Quest. Bk. ii, Ch. iv, pp. 247-9.

"Let us enquire more deeply into this subject. All
bodies must be in motion, or at rest, or in that state in
which by their *vis inertiae* they are resisting any tendency
to change. With respect to the universe, all bodies may
be said to be in motion; while, relatively to ourselves and
to surrounding objects, there are many which appear to be
in repose. It is, however, true that every particle, or
primary atom, in a body said to be at rest, must act, and be
acted upon. Each attracts, or repels, or presses upon that
which is contiguous with it. This may be asserted of every
particle that floats in the air or in the ocean, as well as of
every grain of granite that is compressed in the rock. The
effects of these active powers in bodies are apparently, but
not really, suspended, while each seems to retain its peculiar
form and situation. A stone presses upon the earth, which
sustains and resists it. Every particle in the stone contri-
butes not only to the action of the whole body, in pressing
upon the earth, but also to its continual reaction; and each
atom in the stone resists others like itself, just as the stone
and the earth act and react upon each other. As, however,
the stone, and all the particles which it contains, thus resist,
and are resisted without changing their relative positions,
we say, that their forces are equally poised against each
other, or are *in nisu.*

"In the formation of all material beings the contiguous primary particles must come within the spheres of each other's attraction. When bodies suffer dissolution, their constituent particles must be mutually repelled, and must enter into new combinations. During the period that any being preserves a distinct existence, the attracting and repelling powers in the atoms of which it is composed, are so balanced, as to render it necessary, that every constituent part of the system should still retain its relative situation with respect to the rest. In this manner all bodies are formed, all are preserved, and all are dissolved.

"Now in all these various states of its existence, matter is always obedient to the laws of its own being. Atoms combine, adhere, or separate, and worlds which are composed of atoms, attract or repel each other, while nature still pursues her unalterable path, according to necessity. There is, really, therefore, no such thing as disorder in the natural world. *Chaque être particulier*, says a celebrated French author, *agit toujours dans l'ordre*; *toutes ses actions, tout le système de ses mouvemens, sont toujours une suite necessaire de sa façon d'exister durable ou momentanée.* In no way, then, can we suppose the interference of a Providence in sustaining what we call the natural order of the material universe, for we really contemplate nothing in this but a necessary *series* of changes, which result only from the properties of matter itself."

Ibid., p. 254.

"The distinction, which is made between the moral and physical being of man, has no foundation in the nature of things. Each individual makes a whole in itself, and is a single creature. All the passions, affections, sentiments,

and feelings of men are as much determined by their
physical organization, as is their strength, their appearance, or their stature. The same necessity, which gives
us a peculiar form and constitution, also gives us a
peculiar disposition and character. It is according to the
formation of your eye that you see; and it is according to
the arrangement of the particles in your brain that you
perceive, think, judge, and understand. The moral being
cannot be separated from the physical, because whatever
we term soul, or mind, is nothing else than the result of a
natural organized body, and can no more exist, when that
body decays, than its whiteness can remain after the snow
has melted. All beings have a natural impulse to preserve
themselves in the state which is most suitable to them.
Whatever aids them in this is agreeable to them; and whatever opposes them in it, occasions them pain. The preser-
vation of life, the enjoyment of its pleasures, the secure
possession of the means by which want is removed and
luxury indulged, are objects generally desired by men; and
thence spring their notions of moral order, of the fitness of
things, of religious duty, of civil establishment, and of all
the rules and institutions, which have been adopted by
society for public happiness. In the works of nature and
of art, we still behold what is beautiful, or deformed—what
is useful, or unprofitable, as our own feelings of pleasure, or
of pain, and as our own perceptions of convenience, or of
unsuitableness dictate to us. We do not consider that the
eternal nature of things cannot be constituted according to
our sentiments. We forget that all things, and all events—
all causes and effects—all motives and actions, are necessary
in themselves and that while we fancy that we see order or
disorder, we are only influenced by the sentiments which

our nature obliges us to have; by the desire of making all things concur with our own interests, passions, or prejudices; and by the physical construction and constitution of our own bodies."

.   .   .   .

"In cases, indeed, where our notions of order may be traced from principles in nature, we seldom see much difference of opinion among mankind. There are certain energies belonging to the universal substance, which are differently developed in the various forms of matter. Thus there are forces in all bodies, some of which cause them to unite, and others to separate. We call these attraction, affinity, adhesion, repulsion, reaction, resistance; but when applied to sentient beings we vary the names, and denote the same qualities by the words love, friendship, sympathy, hatred, enmity, antipathy; and we say in common language that the former belong to physical, and the latter to moral beings. This distinction, however, only really exists, inasmuch as the same energies are differently developed in organized, and in unorganized bodies. There is likewise a principle common to all individual beings; and that is, an endeavour to continue in their present state of existence, as long as the means are suitable to that end; for no being resigns its present existence, unless when compelled to do so, by the mode of its being becoming unsuitable to its state. This is true whether we speak of the insensible lump of matter, or of man endowed as he is by nature with sense and intelligence. A lifeless stone endeavours to persevere in its state of motion, or rest, and its component particles adhere together, and repel whatever may be destructive of their union, nor can they be forced to separate but by the action of some power yet greater than that by which they have hitherto been combined. A man who has committed suicide has been compelled to do so by motives which he could not resist; for no one has ever desired to die, while the mode of his existence was judged by him to be suitable to its prolongation. Some superior force, proceeding from calamity, from pain, or from disease, must have seemed, at least, to have rendered the means of preserving existence unsuitable, when courage, or despair, has sought refuge in a necessary death. From these observations we may conclude with certainty, that all bodies are capable of being affected by attraction, and repulsion, of making combinations, of suffering dissolution, and that they always strive to persevere in that state in which they are while it is suitable to them. The motions and dispositions, however, of the primary parts, necessarily influence these various energies, and sometimes favour, and sometimes retard, their development; and as the combinations of causes are more complicated, various, and intricate in some bodies than in others, so will be those of the effects. It is thus that sentient and intelligent beings are produced, form a species of themselves, and follow the laws of a nature which is peculiarly their own. They have not only a *conatus* to persevere in their present state of existence, but the consciousness of that state, and the perception of the means which they consider to be most requisite to sustain it. When those means cease to be suitable, or are so perceived by the thinking creature, its dissolution follows. Every human being, by a necessity which is irresistible, must desire to prolong his existence in the way which appears to him to be best adapted to it; nor will he ever seek to relinquish life unless he be deprived of the means of existing in that manner which he believes necessarily to accord with his nature. It is this desire, then, of preserving life, by such means as seem to us to be most convenient, agreeable, and suitable, that determines almost all our opinions of persons and things. It is still this which chiefly influences those minor energies which our constitution develops. Hence arise the various connections in society; as well as the contentions and the jealousies which disturb it. Hence follow the discords and concords—the enmities and friend-ships—the quarrels and reconciliations, which inflict, and which heal, by turns, the wounds of the world. Hence likewise do we learn to form partial notions of virtue and vice, of right and wrong, of truth and falsehood. Whatever tends to preserve man in the situation which his own feel-ings make him believe to be most generally advantageous to his interests is that which he denominates good, wise, and orderly; and whatever may generally contribute to his pleasure or utility is that which he admires as beautiful, or beneficial. He is necessarily compelled to endeavour to persevere in his state of existence, while he thinks he pos-sesses the means of doing so in the manner which is most desirable for him. All his ideas of order, or of disorder, are founded upon this principle; his views of the whole universe which he knows are connected with it; and he affixes terms of reproach and disgust to events and to beings that in the inevitable course of things interfere with his happiness, diminish his enjoyments, or augment his sufferings."

This passage contains a variety of suggestive points. (*a*) It will be sufficient first to quote Shelley's lines:

"Throughout the varied and eternal world
 Soul is the only element, the block
 That for uncounted ages has remained

The moveless pillar of a mountain's weight
Is active living spirit.   Every grain
Is sentient both in unity and part,
And the minutest atom comprehends
A world of loves and hatreds.   These beget
Evil and good: hence truth and falsehood spring;
Hence will and thought and action, all the germs
Of pain or pleasure, sympathy or hate,
That variegate the eternal universe.
Soul is not more polluted than the beams
Of heaven's pure orb ere round their rapid lines
The taint of earth-born atmospheres arise."

(*b*) This very complex passage seems to be well explained by reference to Drummond.   The passage is clearly not Platonism: it cannot be written off, with the facility of a student's essay, as "Shelley's Platonism."   It seems to be taken straight from Drummond, though we make no futile charge of "plagiarism," but consider only Shelley's power to assimilate ideas.   The slight confusion in Drummond, who seems uncertain whether his atoms do or do not "feel" attraction and repulsion, is practically ignored by Shelley. The poet, naturally, gives them the benefit of the doubt! What is more significant is that Shelley follows on at once with social and political relations, exactly in the manner of Drummond.   While Drummond says, "Hence arise the various connections in society, ...contentions . . . . jealousies . . . .discords . . . . concords . . . . hence . . . . truth and falsehood," Shelley says, "These beget evil and good: hence truth and falsehood spring."   Is it chance that the words are identical?   Or that Shelley says, "Hence will and thought and action" while Drummond says, a few lines earlier, "It is thus that sentient and intelligent beings are produced"? We think that the "gentle reader" who compares these two pieces of writing will feel, primarily, how strongly Drummond's statement of universal activity would appeal to Shelley, and then admit that Shelley's lines are actually a reproduction of the contents of this very statement of the case.

(*c*) The last three lines present a different point on which more will be said later. The reason for the presence of the lines here (for their abruptness seems to need a reason) is found in Drummond, p. 172. "When they thought they had discovered mind to be different from body, because it is the source of motion, they still compared it with the rarest elements of matter. Fire, light, and air were long the symbols of the mental principle. . . . . The Gnostics and Eclectics . . . derived their aeons and emanations from the parent of light," etc. In brief, a transition is made from atoms to atomic souls, the "motes" of the Pythagoreans as quoted by Drummond. Soul is therefore really light, or atoms of light, and these atoms combine in different ways to form plant, animal or human souls. Shelley goes one step further: even stones have souls.

(4) Acad. Quest. Bk. ii, Ch. 5, pp. 283 *seq.*

"It is now my intention to examine a system of some mechanical philosophers, who suppose the vital, or animal, spirits to be the immediate instruments by which the soul holds communication with the external world. When a prospect is spread before the eyes, the animal spirits paint it in all its brilliant colours to the soul; and while the air vibrates with music, they repeat with fidelity the harmonious sounds. Again, when we desire to impart our feelings, the service is not less punctually performed. No interval can be traced between volition and expression. The countenance brightens into smiles, or the brow contracts from resentment, as the mandates of the will are announced to the obedient organs. The animal spirits are the ministers of the passions, and express all their transitions. They supply the orator with the means of elocution, and stimulate his tongue to utterance. They collect at the call of the poet, and bear his genius away to the regions of fiction and romance.

"I begin with asking, what is the substance of the animal spirits? Hippocrates, Erasistratus, Asclepiades, and Galen, seem to have thought that they are aerial. Descartes said, they are of pure flame. Newton appears to have believed that they possess the tenuity of light. Bonnet imagined them to resemble fire; and Bossier adopted a more general opinion, when he compared them to the electrical fluid. Where there is only a choice of conjecture, the cautious reasoner will hesitate before he makes any positive conclusion.

"I would next enquire, what are the channels through which the animal spirits are carried? Is it along the sinuous branches of the nerves, that they travel to and from the common *sensorium*? Luwenhoeck pretends to have seen the cavities through which they pass, but Haller candidly confesses that those cavities were invisible to him, which are, indeed, invisible to everybody else. We must, therefore, reject the specious analogy, according to which the brain fluid, continually flowing between the brain and the external organs, has been compared with the blood propelled through the arteries, and returned by the veins to the heart."

Drummond deals at considerable length with the soul and its operations.

(*a*) On p. 101 he comments on the spider's sense of touch and states that the "Mimosa or sensitive plant is well known to possess a singular degree of sensibility." Shelley's views on the sensitive plant need not be quoted.

(*b*) The passages quoted above are very significant.

Shelley writes in *Alastor*, l. 51 *seq.*:

> "Soon the solemn mood
> Of her pure mind kindled through all her frame
> A permeating fire . . . .
> . . . . in their branching veins
> The eloquent blood told an ineffable tale . . . .
> . . . . and saw, by the warm light of their own life
> Her glowing limbs beneath the sinuous veil
> Of woven wind."

In *Prometheus Unbound*, we read:—
> "Child of Light, thy limbs are burning
> Through the vest which seems to hide them,
> As the radiant lines of morning
> Through the clouds, e'er they divide them."[1]

We may notice here that Drummond and Shelley agree in making the animal spirits ministers of the passions; also that Drummond supplies a nice word for a poet when he speaks of the "sinuous branches of the nerves." Shelley preferred "sinuous veil of woven wind," because the whole picture is thus made more "ethereal." However, "branches of the nerves" and "branching veins," come to much the

[1]*Cf.* p. 181, quotation from *Siris.* Also see p. 201.

same thing when we consider that the doctors disagreed about the channels required for the spirits. The common opinion favoured the veins, for the simple reason that the nerves really provided no "channels" at all. It was neurology that ultimately killed pneumatology.

Shelley's very beautiful conception is that of a being essentially, which here also means internally, composed of pure soul. We have already learned that soul is fire or light or both at once. When Shelley says Life of Life he is using the form which denotes pure essence, just as the Christian fathers said "Light of Light." Language can go no further, but the object is made more conceivable by working out the analogy: as, in the case of ordinary mortals, the limbs might be seen through gauze, so in this case the limbs themselves are the outer texture through which the inner form appears.

(5) Acad. Quest., p. 71.

"When I look out of my window, the objects which I see before me, give me notions of concrete quantities. The mind cannot contemplate more than one idea at a time, with whatever rapidity whole trains may pass before it; and a regular *series* of images passes in my imagination, while I survey the prospect before me, and while the neighbouring shores, covered with buildings, gardens, and vineyards, the sea, a remote promontory, and a farther island, fill the painted field of my vision, and successively attract my attention. But all these objects, with their different distances and relative magnitudes, being, as it were, summed up, make me perceptive of the simple mode of duration, which has been called continuous extension."

Ibid., p. 133.

"We have now traced the visible images of things to those which are *painted* on the *retina*. We may suspect, however, that these are no more the objects of vision than the rest, and that they would not be so, even if they were not always inverted. But their being inverted sufficiently proves that they are not the real images which we see."

We now come to some minor points which are interesting for the student of Shelley's language. Drummond was very fond of the idea that things are "painted on the retina," or that the outer world is in fact a "painted field of vision."

Shelley writes in the well-known sonnet:—

"Lift not the painted veil which those who live
   Call life: though unreal shapes be pictured there,
   And it but mimic all we would believe
   With colours idly spread."

This is good Berkeleianism in a sense. It is more intelligible if we follow Drummond and interpret the "painted field of my vision" as life: if the eye saw directly, that is, without a retina, it would see reality and not "secondary qualities dependent on the percipient." The objection that the eye would really see nothing is irrelevant: more than one writer before Shelley toyed with the idea that the intellect might perceive objects as they really are if the eye-cavity was not obstructed by the eye!

(6) Finally some comments must be made on Shelley's attitude toward the world in which we live. Combining Berkeley's ideas as given above with the similar but more "scientific" views of Drummond, we find that the essential

idea is that of One and Many. So far, Platonism. But Platonism disappears when the idea is developed in terms of white light and refracted light. The terrestrial body is like a prism: it comes between us and the original light: it is a refractive medium. Hence we are compelled to experience the illusion of plurality:—

> Life like a dome of many-coloured glass
> Stains the white radiance of eternity.

Here we might remark that "eternity" is made more intelligible if we take it to mean not indefinite time but the One as substance. This would be justified by Drummond's statement (p. 245) that "Parmenides holds that the divine incorporeal substance is, as Cudworth expresses it, a constant, present eternity." In the "Essay on Life,"[1] Shelley wrote: "This logic strips, as it were, the painted curtain from this scene of things," a sentence which shows in a very interesting way how an idea was formulated by Shelley in prose and then moulded to a more exact poetic form.

That Shelley's language was very exact has been noted by Professor Whitehead,[1] and it is the argument of this essay that many phrases which pass for "poetic" or exotic

[1]*Works*, edited H. Buxton Forman Vol. vi, p. 257. See passages quoted above, p. 171-2.

[1]See *Science and the Modern World*, by Professor A. N. Whitehead, p. 119. "For the sake of estimating the value of Shelley's evidence it is important to realise this absorption of his mind in scientific ideas. It can be illustrated by lyric after lyric. I will choose one poem only, the fourth act of his *Promethus Unbound*. The Earth and the Moon converse together in the language of accurate science. Physical experiments guide his imagery. For example, the Earth's exclamation,
'The vaporous exultation not to be confined!'
is the poetic transcript of 'the expansive force of gases,' . . . . ."
as it is termed in books on science.

groups of words are really very precise applications of scientific ideas. In this connection I revert to the passage quoted on p. 197 above. Here Shelley is working with another of his central concepts, namely, that the earth is surrounded by an atmosphere through which pure light passes and is refracted. Hence the passage means:—The soul (in itself, without the refractive medium of its body) is as pure as the sun's rays before they become refracted by the atmosphere through which they pass to us. It is this terrestrial density which makes the painted veil in general. This also explains the couplet in *Prometheus Unbound* (205), where the voice from the air says:

"I had clothed, since Earth uprose,
Its wastes in colours not their own."

What the usual interpretation of this passage is, I do not know: it is probably taken to be pure exuberance of language. But in the light of what has been said about Shelley's Newtonian bias and his persistent use of the idea of prismatic colours, it seems to express precisely the function of the air, or "earth-born atmospheres," to produce those colours which would otherwise not exist and cannot be found above in "the white radiance of eternity."

CONCLUSION

To avoid misconception, and especially to obviate the idea that this essay is meant to prove in a mean spirit that Shelley has been detected in the act of copying Sir William Drummond, the conclusion may be summarily stated. The essay has attempted to show, on a larger scale, the meaning of the statement that Shelley adopted the "immaterial philosophy." The term immaterial is rather misleading. The philosophy was a view of life akin to that of Berkeley and even more closely related to that of Drummond. Drummond was not the author of a philosophy but the exponent of a theory which grew, as did Berkeley's philosophy, from conceptions of matter and qualities current after Newton's time. Without being directly responsible for the philosophical systems of the eighteenth century, Newton became the source of varied ideas about the physical universe. It is now generally admitted that much so-called Platonism is really Newtonism. The reason for a distinction lies in the fact that emphasis is thrown on light and a language is used which could not antedate Newton's optics. It seems that our valuation of Shelley as an accurate thinker and our interpretation of his language can be improved by realizing this fact. It is hardly necessary to add that Shelley had other interests and that much of his writing is not directly affected by these considerations.

INHIBITIONS OF BROWNING'S POETRY

J. F. Macdonald

IN *An Essay on Shelley* Browning divides poets into two
great classes, objective and subjective, the objective
poet "choosing to deal with the doings of men," the subjective, "whose study has been himself," preferring "to
dwell upon those external scenic appearances which strike
out most abundantly and uninterruptedly his inner light
and power." There is no uncertainty about Browning's
class. Even in *Pauline*, his earliest poem that we have,
he speaks of his plan "to look on real life," to learn "mankind, its cares, hopes, fears, its woes and joys"; in *How it
Strikes a Contemporary* of 1855, the poet is God's reporter,
setting down for his Master's conning every least bit of
human behaviour that might have significance. And in
House, published in 1876, Browning has a fling at the reve-
lations of the subjective poet. The closing stanza is well-
known:

> "Hoity-toity! a street to explore,
>   Your house the exception! *'With this same key
> Shakespeare unlocked his heart'*, once more!"
>   Did Shakespeare? If so, the less Shakespeare he!

The owner of the house had lived in decent reticence till an
earthquake shaved the front sheer off, crushed him in the
ruins, and left the rooms gaping for the gaze of the inquisi-
tive. It will take another earthquake to bare the inner
rooms of Browning's house. He warns the reader that the
most to be had is

> A peep through my window, if folk prefer;
>> But, please you, no foot over threshold of mine!

And he adds almost angrily,

> Outside should suffice for evidence:
> And whoso desires to penetrate
> Deeper, must dive by the spirit-sense—
> No optics like yours, at any rate!"—

a challenge, one feels sure, that will set many a psycho-analyst diving into these murky waters.

Evidently when Browning wrote this provoking little poem at the age of sixty-four he had a comfortable feeling that the windows were closed and the blinds drawn in the house of his spirit. Peering eyes had not seen whatever he chose to keep secret behind the curtains. And the curtains had never been up when the lights were lit in the house. He protested again and again at the habit people had of accepting as his the opinions he put into the mouths of characters in his poems. The group of poems entitled *Men and Women*, he declared with emphasis, expressed only the opinions of so many imaginary persons. The commentators have refused to believe him and will tell you just what Browning thought about a host of things that range from the joy of man's life here to the certainty of his life here-after. On these points they quote you passages, pat to the purpose, from *Saul* and *A Grammarian's Funeral*, two poems from that very volume of *Men and Women* that Browning had described as "so many utterances of so many imaginary persons, not mine." Which is right, the poet or the commentator?

It is rather strange that Browning should be so sensitive

about revealing his thoughts and feelings. For certainly this almost morbid reticence is no mark of objective poets as a class. Chaucer is quite as objective a poet as Browning. Dare we say "the less Chaucer he" because we see his eyes twinkle when he gravely agrees with the monk's opinion of work and strict monastic rules, or grow dim with unshed tears when he pays tribute to his good 'persoune' who, in those hard days after the ravages of the Black Death, stuck to his post of Christ's shepherd and "coude in litel thynge have sufficaunce." Isn't he the most delectable of poets just because he lays bare his feelings before us, indeed is almost unconscious of us in his healthy outlook on that busy world of ever-interesting men and women? No inhibitions in his sub-conscious soul make us "dive by the spirit-sense" to penetrate the mystery of his inner thoughts and feelings.

It occurred to me that the place to look for evidence as to the success with which Browning kept the world outside his threshold was in those poems where he was confessedly speaking in his own person. In the first place this non-dramatic, or as Browning would call it, subjective verse is a very small part of the vast bulk of his poetry, over 1,000 pages close printed in double column in the single volume editions. Even if we include a good many poems that Browning himself put among his dramatic lyrics, dramatic romances, or *Dramatis Personae* and two long poems *La Saisiaz* and *Christmas Eve and Easter Day*, which are certainly dramatic in parts,—even then we can only compile just over 60 pages. If we omit the two long poems, there are less than 35 pages in which Browning even tells a story in his own person. That is actually a smaller space than the non-dramatic poems occupy in Shakespeare's work.

In the second place, quite half of these 35 pages have little significance, being filled for the most part with what are conveniently classed as occasional poems. In the 70's and 80's when Browning was a literary lion in London he was constantly besought for these occasional verses. So we have his Goldoni sonnet, and the sonnet entitled *The Names*, written for the Shakespearean Show-Book, the *Epitaph on Levi Lincoln Thaxter,* the lines to the musician, Mr. Arthur Chappell, and half a dozen more little poems of the same slight kind. *Cenciaja* is a bit of versified history adding an interesting detail to the story of Beatrice Cenci's execution. *The Guardian Angel* is mere description of a painting by Guercino, written for his friend Domett whose sudden leaving London for New Zealand in 1842 was the occasion of *Waring*, written in whimsical mock-heroic style that half conceals its depth of affection. *Tray* is a libel on the vivisectionists. *Sibrandus Schnafaburgensis* is an amusing tirade against pedantry, and *Old Pictures in Florence*, though acute and interesting art criticism, is put in the form of his outburst of humorous vexation as an unlucky collector of old masters. *Transcendentalism* is good-natured advice to a young poet against writing a long subjective poem, *Memorabilia* an exquisite and delicate tribute to his beloved Shelley, as *Popularity* is a more laboured one to Keats. *The Lost Leader* is his vigorous denunciation of Wordsworth for having abandoned his earlier liberal principles, "just for a handful of silver", as he unjustly charged. Clearly there is nothing in any of these poems to need the veil of reticence.

The other subjective poems fall into three groups: (1) poems in praise of England, (2) poems with Mrs. Browning as their theme, and (3) poems that express ideas on matters of conduct or belief.   There is no trace of hesitation or self-consciousness in the first two of these groups.   Of course one is expected to love his country and his wife and to take no shame for saying so, though English custom is to protest one's love in public sparingly and seldom.   The patriotic verse is sparse enough—a few lines in *Pauline*, the toast to Nelson's memory that forms the third section of *Nationality in Drinks*, and the famous *Home Thoughts from Abroad* and *Home Thoughts from the Sea*.   I suppose no poem of Browning's is better known or better loved than the first of this pair, the rippling lines,

> Oh, to be in England
> Now that April's there,

the most musical lyric he ever wrote.

Mrs. Browning is the inspiration of so many of Browning's poems that it is quite difficult to be sure one's list is inclusive.   Mrs. Sutherland Orr, for instance, maintains that Pompilia is very definitely based on the personality of Mrs. Browning.   But everyone will agree that *My Star*, *One Word More*, *Prospice*, The Invocation in *The Ring and the Book* beginning "Oh Lyric Love, half angel and half bird" and *By the Fireside* have her as their central theme.   Those familiar with Browning need no reminding of the peculiar intensity and passion of these lyrics.   They seem to be written for her eyes alone though published for all the world to read as if Browning gloried in having been the one to whom she gave her heart.

There is a curious difference in the third group, the group that touches on matters of conduct or belief.   First consider a judgment on conduct.   Browning, I imagine, is still quoted oftener than any other poet by clergymen, but I have never heard one refer to the closing stanzas of *The Statue and the Bust*, in which Browning condemns the dilatory lovers who hadn't the moral courage to break convention and commit in deed the sin they dwelt on in imagination.   There may be just a touch of bravado in the closing challenge but one can't help feeling the power and sincerity of his judgment on the futile pair:

> The counter our lovers staked was lost
> As surely as if it were lawful coin:
> And the sin I impute to each frustrate ghost
>
> Is—the unlit lamp and the ungirt loin,
> Though the end in sight was a vice, I say.
> You of the virtue (we issue join)
> How strive you?   *De te, fabula!*

The only hint of self-consciousness in these stanzas is the sense of running counter to convention in

> You of the virtue (we issue join)
> How strive you?   *De te, fabula!*

as who should say with a toss of his head, "Put that in your pipe and smoke it."

In *Shop*, Browning criticizes the man whose shop was all his house, the man who lived meanly in a cubby hole behind his place of business lest he might miss a possible sale.   He concludes this poem, quite characteristic in its vivid descriptive phrases, with two stanzas that have been repeatedly laughed at and parodied, especially the first of the two. Indeed it reads like a parody itself:

I want to know a butcher paints,
  A baker rhymes for his pursuit,
Candlestick-maker much acquaïnts
  His soul with song, or haply mute,
  Blows out his brains upon the flute!

But—shop each day and all day long!
  Friend, your good angel slept, your star
Suffered eclipse, fate did you wrong!
  From where these sorts of treasures are,
  There should our hearts be—Christ, how far!

To my ear something rings false in this little poem.   To put the kindest interpretation on it, Browning seems only half in earnest.   The rapid movement of the verse with its jigging rhymes gives an almost ridiculous tone.   How different is Emerson's sober way of putting the same thing, when he says that a man "should not be merely a farmer, but a man farming."   The difference is even greater in the passage of scripture that Browning evidently had in mind, "Where a man's treasure is, there will his heart be also." Yet unless Browning felt embarrassed at offering any criticism or advice on conduct, one finds it hard to see why he couldn't state this little commonplace of morality more effectively.   Strange as it seemed, these were the only passages I could find in which Browning, in his own person, commented on matters of conduct.   Neither one of them has that freedom from self-consciousness which is the hallmark of perfect sincerity.

He speaks in his own person on religious questions in a bare dozen poems.   *Fears and Scruples* in the *Pacchiarotto* volume of 1876 proved so puzzling with its crabbed phraseology, frequent parentheses, and involved syntax that

Browning felt it necessary to write a letter of explanation. At that I think the poem is simpler than the letter. But *Fears and Scruples*, as anyone can see who chooses to read it, is a curious and tortuous expression of a puzzled and irritated mind. The very metre with its queer half-comic rhymes creates an impression of insincerity, as if the writer were merely playing with his serious subject.

All the other poems of the group deal in one form or other with the question of immortality, in Browning's mind the one vital question in religion. In the Epilogue to *Fifine at the Fair*, he treats it in a kind of allegory, with a sub-title of *The Householder*:

I.

Savage I was sitting in my house, late, lone:
    Dreary, weary with the long day's work:
Head of me, heart of me, stupid as a stone:
    Tongue-tied now, now blaspheming like a Turk;
When, in a moment, just a knock, call, cry,
    Half a pang and all a rapture, there again were we!—
"What, and is it really you again?" quoth I:
    "I again, what else did you expect?" quoth She.

II.

"Never mind, hie away from this old house—
    Every crumbling brick embrowned with sin and
    shame!
Quick, in its corners ere certain shapes arouse!
    Let them—every devil of the night—lay claim,
Make and mend, or rap and rend, for me! Good-bye!
    God be their guard from disturbance at their glee,
Till, crash, comes down the carcass in a heap!" quoth I:
    "Nay, but there's a decency required!" quoth She.

III.

"Ah, but if you knew how time has dragged, days,
  nights!
  All the neighbour-talk with man and maid—such
  men!
All the fuss and trouble of street-sounds, window-
  sights:
  All the worry of flapping door and echoing roof; and
  then,
All the fancies. . . . . Who were they had leave, dared
  try
  Darker arts that almost struck despair in me?
If you knew but how I dwelt down here!" quoth I:
  "And was I so better off up there?" quoth She.

IV.

"Help and get it over! *Reunited to his wife*
  (How draw up the paper lets the parish-people
  know?)
Lies M., or N., departed from this life,
  Day the this or that, month and year the so and so.
What i' the way of final flourish? Prose, verse? Try!
  Affliction sore long time he bore, or, what is it to be?
Till God did please to grant him ease. Do end!" quoth I:
  "I end with—Love is all, and Death is nought!"
  quoth She.

Again one feels a lack of perfect sincerity, probably
because of the jigging metre and the nervous giggle in that
last stanza. I submit that is not the way to state one's
convictions on a matter as important, literally, as life and

death. To resurrect a useful phrase of Matthew Arnold's
it has not the accent of high seriousness which the subject
demands.

The Prologue to *Pacchiarotto* is another half allegory
more simply stated:

I.

Oh, the old wall here!   How I could pass
  Life in a long midsummer day,
My feet confined to a plot of grass,
  My eyes from a wall not once away!

II.

And lush and lithe do the creepers clothe
  Yon wall I watch, with a wealth of green:
Its bald red bricks draped, nothing loth,
  In lappets of tangle they laugh between.

III.

Now, what is it makes pulsate the robe?
  Why tremble the sprays?   What life o'erbrims
The body,—the house, no eye can probe,—
  Divined as, beneath a robe, the limbs?

IV.

And there again! But my heart may guess
  Who tripped behind; and she sang perhaps:
So, the old wall throbbed, and its life's excess
  Died out and away in the leafy wraps!

V.

Wall upon wall are between us: life
  And song should away from heart to heart!
I—prison-bird, with a ruddy strife
  At breast, and a lip whence storm-notes start—

VI.

Hold on, hope hard in the subtle thing
  That's spirit: though cloistered fast, soar free;
Account as wood, brick, stone, this ring
  Of the rueful neighbours, and—forth to thee!

Note that here he is a prison-bird, with a ruddy strife at
breast, that he holds on, hopes hard in the subtle thing
that's spirit and in spirit fares "forth to thee." Isn't the
statement of belief more convincing here just because we
feel it is made with fuller conviction? Is it not fair to say
that the conviction is fuller because the belief is less?

At any rate the acquiescence in what may be the end of
it all—rest in the quiet grave—has given an accent of full
sincerity to the exquisite little poem in *Jocoseria* of 1883:

Never the time and the place
  And the loved one all together!
This path—how soft to pace!
  This May—what magic weather!
Where is the loved one's face?
In a dream that loved one's face meets mine,
  But the house is narrow, the place is bleak
Where, outside, rain and wind combine
  With a furtive ear, if I strive to speak,

With a hostile eye at my flushing cheek,
With a malice that marks each word, each sign!
O enemy sly and serpentine,
   Uncoil thee from the waking man!
      Do I hold the Past
      Thus firm and fast
Yet doubt if the Future hold I can?
This path so soft to pace shall lead
Thro' the magic of May to herself indeed!
Or narrow if needs the house must be,
Outside are the storms and strangers: we—
Oh, close, safe, warm sleep I and she,
—I and she!

There isn't yet quite the full resignation, indeed almost the
feeling of relief, that Hardy makes the elderly widow voice
in *She Hears the Storm*.   As she listens to the rain thudding
on the thatch, she recalls her old anxiety that is now gone,
for the husband about whom she used to worry

> '. . has won that storm-tight roof of hers
> Which Earth grants all her kind.'

Browning never acquiesced, whatever he may have come
to believe, but unless my spirit-sense is not attuned to catch
the messages from his, he writes more freely and sincerely
when his head and heart are not at war.   And they are at
war whenever he touches on problems of religious faith.
Take the *Christmas Eve and Easter Day* written in 1850 in
the early years of his happy marriage.   As Griffin and
Minchin point out in *The Life of Robert Browning* (p. 172):

"Those who would deduce from this poem, or rather pair
of poems, a precise conclusion as to their author's religious

belief are confronted by an initial difficulty. There is no apparent reason why the narrator in *Christmas Eve* should not have also seen the visions described by the chief speaker in *Easter Day*, but Browning is careful to point out that they are two distinct persons:

> "It chanced that I had cause to cross
> The common, where the chapel was,
> Our friend spoke of, the other day."

There is also the third character—*Easter Day* being a dialogue—to be reckoned with; and he is by no means in accord with the seer of visions. The poems, therefore, are "dramatic," and it is consequently unsafe to identify Browning with any of his three characters."

Certainly the only one of the three with whom he could be identified is the speaker in *Christmas Eve*. The conclusion is well-known: the speaker gives up both the Pope with his buffoonery and the Göttingen professor with his rationalism for the bare little church of his vision:

> Meantime, in the still recurring fear
>   Lest myself, at unawares, be found,
>   While attacking the choice of my neighbours round,
> With none of my own made—I choose here!
> The giving out of the hymn reclaims me;
> I have done: and if any blames me,
> Thinking that merely to touch in brevity
>   The topics I dwell on, were unlawful,—
> Or worse, that I trench, with undue levity,
>   On the bounds of the holy and the awful,—
> I praise the heart, and pity the head of him,
> And refer myself to **THEE**, instead of him,

> Who head and heart alike discernest,
>> Looking below light speech we utter,
>> When frothy spume and frequent sputter
> Prove that the soul's depths boil in earnest!

With that metre jigging in our ears, it is easy to understand why the reviewer in the *Athenaeum*, while admitting the beauty of many isolated passages, deprecated the discussion of religious questions in what he termed "doggerel verse." Yet the quality of the verse is quite as good as that of the discussion, which merely plays with the subject and comes to no conclusion except the "I choose here," a choice for which no reason is stated.

Finally consider *La Saisïaz*, the poem in memory of his friend, Miss Egerton Smith, who died suddenly in the autumn of 1877 when staying with Browning and his sister at a little villa, La Saisïaz, four or five miles from Geneva. Browning, on going to waken her in the morning for a trip they had planned up the mountain, found her dead. She and Browning, a few days before her death, had been discussing the question of immortality, a topic that was the subject of a symposium then running in the *Nineteenth Century*. It is natural that her death should bring the problem before him with peculiar vividness. But even in these circumstances he does not discuss the question directly. He has Fancy and Reason hold debate, with Reason having the last word and Browning as arbiter giving judgment at the end:

> So, I hope—no more than hope, but hope—no less than
>> hope, because
> I can fathom, by no plumb-line sunk in life's apparent
>> laws,

How I may in any instance fix where change should
  meetly fall
Nor involve, by one revisal, abrogation of them all:
—Which again involves as utter change in life thus
  law-released,
Whence the good of goodness vanished when the ill of
  evil ceased.
Whereas, life and laws apparent re-instated,—all we
  know,
All we know not,—o'er our heaven again cloud closes,
  until, lo,—
Hope the arrowy, just as constant, comes to pierce its
  gloom, compelled
By a power and by a purpose which, if no one else
  beheld,
I behold in life, so—hope!

That is the point he had reached in the autumn of 1877 and
the reader will recall the even soberer utterance of 1883 in
Never the time and the place and the loved one all together.

Now it is quite true there is direct testimony that
Browning professed a firm belief in immortality. Professor
Knight, for example, reports him saying, "As to immortality, I don't need arguments, I know it by intuition,
which is superior to proof." And Griffin and Minchin quote
a letter of 1876, written in reply to one from a lady who,
"believing herself to be dying, wrote to thank him for the
help she had derived from his poems, mentioning particularly *Rabbi Ben Ezra* and *Abt Vogler*." It is significant
that his letter says not a word about these or indeed about
any other of his own poems. "It is a great thing, the
greatest, that a human being should have passed the pro-

bation of life, and sum up its experience in a witness to the power and love of God. I dare congratulate you. All the help I can offer, in my poor degree, is the assurance that I see ever *more* reason to hold by the same hope—and that by no means in ignorance of what has been advanced to the contrary; and for your sake I could wish it to be true that I had so much of 'genius' as to permit the testimony of an especially privileged insight to come in aid of the ordinary argument. For I know I, myself, have been aware of the communication of something more subtle than a ratiocinative process, when the convictions of 'genius' have thrilled my soul to its depths, as when Napoleon, shutting up the New Testament, said of Christ: 'Do you know that I am an understander of men? Well, He was no man!' Or when Charles Lamb, in a gay fancy with some friends as to how he and they would feel if the greatest of the dead were to appear suddenly in flesh and blood once more, on the final suggestion, 'And if Christ entered this room?' changed his manner at once, and stuttered out, as his manner was when moved, 'You see, if Shakespeare entered,' we should all rise; if *He* appeared, we must kneel.' Or, not to multiply instances, as when Dante wrote what I will transcribe from my wife's Testament wherein I recorded it fourteen years ago, 'Thus I believe, thus I affirm, thus I am certain it is, that from this life I shall pass to another, there, where that lady lives of whom my soul was enamoured.' Dear friend, I may have wearied you in spite of your good will. God bless you, sustain, and receive you?"

There is the statement, too, in *Epilogue* that ended his last volume:

Held we fall to rise, are baffled to fight better,
    Sleep to wake.

. . . . . .

"Strive and thrive!" cry "Speed,—fight on, fare ever
    There as here!"

It is clear that Browning had the will to believe and did
in fact believe in immortality. But the thing that warped
his poetry was another fact, namely, his irritation of spirit
at not being able to justify his faith to his reason. In the
words of his Bishop Blougram he had "a life of faith diver-
sified by doubt", and perhaps would accept the definition
he puts into the Bishop's mouth,

With me, faith means perpetual unbelief
Kept quiet like the snake 'neath Michael's foot
Who stands calm just because he feels it writhe.

That Browning felt it writhe and did not stand calm there is
plenty of evidence. First of all is that remarkable poem
Pauline, which he tried so hard to keep hidden and apolo-
gized for so needlessly when he reprinted it in a collected
edition in 1867, thirty-four years after it had been printed
anonymously and not a copy sold. This poem, written
when he was a young man of twenty-one, seems to me a
genuine bit of spiritual autobiography, and I can claim in
support of this view the weighty authority of John Stuart
Mill as well as of Griffin and Minchin, who say that his
reluctance to reprint it was owing to the fact that "dramatic
as he had intended his poem to be, there was only too much
of self-revelation in its pages" and that "it must be accepted
in its main outlines as distinctly autobiographical, and, if
read aright, as the most authentic record of his early life."

The nature of this self-revelation is well stated by Mill in the note he made at the end of the volume sent him by Fox:

"With considerable poetic powers, the writer seems to me possessed with a more intense and morbid self-consciousness than I ever knew in any sane human being. I should think it a sincere confession, though of a most unlovable state, if the 'Pauline' were not evidently a mere phantom. All about her is full of inconsistency—he neither loves her nor fancies he loves her, yet insists upon *talking* love to her. . . . He is evidently *dissatisfied*, and feels part of the badness of his state; he does not write as if it were purged out of him. If he once could muster a hearty hatred of his selfishness it would *go*; as it is, he feels only the *lack* of *good*, not the positive evil. He feels not remorse, but only disappointment; a mind in that state can only be regenerated by some new passion, and I know not what to wish for him but that he may meet with a *real* Pauline."

In the second place there is a mass of testimony that Browning, though a great talker, persistently declined to discuss matters of belief except with a very few intimate friends. The reason, I think, is clear. Even so friendly a critic and interpreter as Henry Jones in his *Browning as a Philosophical and Religious Teacher* points out that the defect of Browning's teaching is its failure to reconcile his heart and head. One can't reason about an intuition. Moreover the time-spirit was against him. Science, triumphant and a bit arrogant, was making men feel, with Huxley, that the word "miracle" was a contradiction in terms. Strauss, Mill, George Eliot, Matthew Arnold, Comte, Spencer—they were all against him, and the Positivists came to possess the earth. Now a man of Browning's active and vigorous mind could not help being affected by the religious controversies of his time. That he knew all the arguments pro and con is abundantly clear from poems like *Bishop Blougram*, *Christmas Eve*, *Easter Day*, and *La Saisïaz*. Cardinal Wiseman, in his review of *Men and Women* in the *Rambler*, acutely remarked about *Bishop Blougram*, "If Mr. Browning is a man of will and action, and not a mere dreamer and talker, we should never feel surprise at his conversion." But Browning couldn't follow Newman on the road to Rome and to reliance on authority any more than he could feel wholly at ease in his belief based on intuition. Hence came the conflict in his spirit, hidden, so far as he could hide it, from the eyes of the world. On the one side were the evangelical piety of his mother, the intense, half-mystical spiritualism of Mrs. Browning, and his own passionate longing for a continuance of this life which he enjoyed with such zest; on the other, the corroding criticism of his time gradually eating away the bulwarks of the older faith.

And so Browning can speak with perfect sincerity of conviction only when he is the spiritual medium for some one else, only when he is voicing the opinion of some imaginary person, not his own. His invention of the dramatic monologue was a necessity of the spirit if he were to write with his full power. Just recall a few of these great utterances. Cleon writes to the king:

> I dare at times imagine to my need
> Some future state revealed to us by Zeus,
> Unlimited in capability
> For joy, as this is in desire for joy,
> —To seek which, the joy hunger forces us:

and Karshish, smitten with the sudden revelation that the God of Power may be also the God of Love, writes to his master Abib as his colour heightens with excitement:

> The very God! think, Abib; dost thou think?
> So, the All-Great, were the All-Loving too—
> So, through the thunder comes a human voice
> Saying, "O heart I made, a heart beats here!
> "Face, my hands fashioned, see it in myself!
> "Thou hast no power nor mayst conceive of mine,
> "But love I gave thee, with myself to love,
> "And thou must love me who have died for thee!"
> The madman saith He said so: it is strange.

And finally that glorious call of the old Rabbi Ben Ezra with its serene confidence in the uses of the master's cup:

> Grow old along with me!
> The best is yet to be,
> The last of life, for which the first was made:
> Our times are in His hand
> Who saith, "A whole I planned,
> Youth shows but half; trust God: see all nor be afraid!"

Why is there no such lyrical outburst in the subjective poems? Is it not because Browning, an able, passionate, and honest man—but with intense and morbid self-consciousness—feels perfectly free to voice these opinions of Cleon, Karshish, and Rabbi Ben Ezra in full sincerity? But just what are his own beliefs? Is he perfectly sure that he holds as full truth exactly what he is saying? At once he becomes self-conscious and puts on the protective armour of a jigging metre or flippant manner, and sincerity and simplicity are gone. Except in a few poems to Mrs.

Browning, where a yearning that is almost agony gives him a momentary fullness of faith, he has written nothing in his own personality that is at all comparable to the great utterances of the host of persons he has created and made voice his deepest longings and aspirations.   He could express himself with perfect sincerity only through the spiritual medium of another personality because he had never wholly reconciled his head and his heart.   That to my spirit-sense is the fatal inhibition in the subjective poetry of Browning.

THE FRENCH REPUTATION OF MATTHEW ARNOLD*

E. K. Brown

AMONG the laws of the science of comparative literature none is more nearly certain than that which I shall illustrate in this account of the French reputation of Matthew Arnold. The law in point states that what one people seeks in the culture of another is not the reflection of its own genius but the impact of something evidently alien. Prince Mirsky gave an admirable illustration of the operation of this law when he explained the Occidental indifference to the greatest figure in Russian literature. "Few foreigners" he says, "have been able to understand the Russian attitude towards Pushkin. Still fewer have found it possible to place him, as the Russians do, among the greatest poets of all nations. Though he is the most universal and the most European of Russian writers, he is still the divinity of a strictly national cult. This sounds paradoxical but is only natural. The foreign reader values Russian writers for what he thinks are their most Russian qualities—qualities which he cannot find anywhere else. Russian literature is still exotic to the rest of Europe and prized in the measure of its obvious originality." It is not unnatural, then, following Prince Mirsky, that where Tolstoy finds hundreds of readers and Dostoievsky scores, Pushkin goes unread and almost untranslated. Now of the

*For their kindness in indicating some of the sources of information on which I have drawn in this article, I wish to thank MM. Baldensperger, Cazamian and E. Guyot of the Sorbonne, M. A. Debailleul of the Lycée Louis-le-Grand (Paris) and M. Louis Bonnerot of the Lycée at Amiens.

four major Victorian prophets,—Carlyle, Newman, Arnold and Ruskin,—Arnold alone was clearly aware of the past and present of France, Arnold alone was an advocate for the adoption in England of French standards, Arnold alone incurred the charge of spiritual expatriation, of becoming, in Sir Walter Raleigh's sneering phrase, "a well-bred, highly cultivated stranger." Carlyle, who saw nothing in the tragedies of Racine and strange inexistent things in the French Revolution, has found sympathetic French interpreters through whose glosses he has been a real if minor influence upon French literature and politics. The most discerning critic of Newman, who was as English as beef and beer, is a French priest. And Ruskin, for whom France was chiefly a matter of cathedrals and castles, was the object of a cult among certain of the literary chapels of the last generation. All three have been widely read in France; all three have been the subjects of careful biographical and critical studies. There are, besides, long books on the French reputation of Carlyle and Ruskin; and an elaborate study of the French reputation of Newman is in progress. How different has been the lot of Arnold, the intention of all whose criticism was, as Mr. T. S. Eliot has put it, "to build a bridge across the Channel."

I. EARLY JUDGMENTS

The first French notice of Matthew Arnold, an article in his adored *Revue des deux mondes*, appeared in mid-September, 1854. This was a review of *Empedocles on Etna* and the *Poems* of 1853, the work of one Arthur Dudley, a teacher in Paris and a copious contributor to the review. Dudley couples Arnold with the "spasmodic" poet Alexander Smith, by means of a surprising and quite illusory filiation from Shelley. Neither relationship could give anything but pain and annoyance to Arnold who, in fact, voiced his disappointment in a contemporary letter, published in Mr. Whitridge's selection.

The cardinal claim of the review, Arnold's descent from Shelley, if untenable, is nevertheless suggestive. Shelley, the ingenious reviewer says, was a centre and a source because his dazzling genius was fortified by powerful convictions and dignified by a lofty character. His work called for completion, however, because he was shut out from truth by an invincible pride and a taste for blasphemy and negation. Arnold shared with Shelley, as with Goethe, a refined artistic consciousness, a need for pure austere structure, a dominant devotion to the Greek ideal. In the place of Shelley's blasphemies and negations, Arnold offered a curiosity which condemns nothing but tends rather to elicit from all the phenomena of life their distinct irreplaceable iotas of significance. He seeks with grave enthusiasm (the reviewer suggests) to pass from the visible isolated outposts of truth to its sanctum. In a vivid prophetic sentence Dudley pictures Arnold as "turning with outstretched arms toward the impenetrable and casting forth from the darkness of human life the appeal of Goethe's Titans: "Give me light, give me more and more light." The substance of *The Scholar-Gipsy*, still unwritten, could not be better indicated.

It is improbable that Shelley was ever a determining or even a modifying factor in Arnold's development. Once when he was aiming at insult, he alluded to Swinburne as "a pseudo-Shelley"; and Swinburne, who was a perspicacious critic in little things as well as in large, did not take this for a compliment. The review of Dowden's *Life of*

Shelley has lost Arnold many a disciple; and the avuncular complacence of the passage in the paper on Byron where he pats Shelley on his curls as "a beautiful and ineffectual angel beating in the void his luminous wings in vain" does not display that "reverence which we owe to founders" which Arnold preached and loyally practised.

Nevertheless this article of Dudley has the prestige of "how it strikes a contemporary." And one who applies its suggestions will arrive at hitherto unsupposed likenesses between the two philosophic lyrists, both seekers of absolute values, both lovers of primitive nature and simple womanhood, both overcome by a tremulous melancholy.

In the course of his examination of the preface to the *Poems* of 1853, Dudley makes a really astonishing prophecy:

"I am much mistaken," he says, "if his fine critical prose will not some day prove how little lyrical form matters to the complete expression of his mind. Rhythm is almost a fetter to Mr. Arnold. Prose adapts itself so neatly to his clear and ordered flow of ideas, it suffices so admirably for the expression of his decisive intelligence, that one wonders whether it is not his genuine mode of expression, the mode to which he will later adhere."

Here is compensation for whatever misguided ingenuity mars the body of the article! May Arthur Dudley have his critical immortality by this one prevision!

In 1860, Matthew Arnold's poetry was brought to the notice of the French public by Sainte-Beuve. In preparing for the press lectures delivered at Liège during the lean year of 1848, on the subject, *Chateaubriand et son groupe littéraire sous l'empire,* he added as his only intercalation a translation in verse of *Obermann*. This translation he ascribes in great part to Auguste Lacaussade, a pensive charming lyrist still remembered and read in France; and thus he paves the way for a record of Arnold's polite profession that he prefers the translation to the original since the former celebrates Obermann in the language that he himself spoke and wrote. Sainte-Beuve gives us two important facts relative to the poem's composition: it was written in the autumn of 1849 and it was an expression of Arnold's unrest before the prospect of a life of action. "Mr. Matthew Arnold," says the prince of critics, "travelling in Switzerland and following in Obermann's footsteps, dedicated to him a poem in which all of Obermann is evoked and in which the poet says farewell to the great dreamer and thinker before his return to take up a life of action." In a note he takes his leave of Arnold's poem, aptly praising it as "an immortal funeral wreath." The year before, during his educational mission to France, Arnold had seen a good deal of Sainte-Beuve; and it was probably during their conversations, which sometimes ran on to midnight, that Sainte-Beuve learned of Arnold's poem. Arnold was exultant when he read Saint-Beuve's comment upon it. "I value his praise," he exclaims, "both in itself and because it carries one's name through the literary circles of Europe in a way that no English praise can carry it. But apart from that, to anyone but a glutton of praise the whole value of it lies in the mode in which it is administered; and this is administered by the first of living critics and with a delicacy for which we would look in vain here."

Essays in Criticism and *Lectures on Translating Homer* were the subject of an article in the *Revue des deux mondes* for the first of April, 1866. Louis Etienne, professor of

philosophy at the great Parisian *lycée* of Saint-Louis, and a
hellenist of mark, was its author.   He repels the suggestion
that Arnold was a disciple of Shelley, and aligns his criticism
with the philosophical efforts of Coleridge and his poetry
with Keats's quest of perfect beauty.   The essay on
Joubert, entitled in its first redaction *Joubert or a French
Coleridge*, and distinguished by eager comprehensive praise
of Coleridge's intelligence, must have led Louis Etienne to
his claim that "after the primary influence of his father, no
other is so evident in Arnold's writings as the influence of
Coleridge."   As one rereads the essay on Joubert, noting
its effect upon this contemporary French reviewer, one
questions whether Arnold should not have included the
name of Coleridge in the company of his teachers thanked
so munificently twenty years later in the discourse on
Emerson.   His conception of the Established Church recalls
Church and State; the experimental method of *Literature
and Dogma* and *God and the Bible* is not easily to be distinguished from the method practised in the *Confessions
of an Inquiring Spirit*; and, finally, Coleridge's discrim-
ination of the imaginative from the fanciful is, obscurely
apprehended and falteringly employed, the touchstone by
which Arnold knows great art from mediocre.

No less arresting is the reviewer's claim that Keats is
among Arnold's ancestors.   "Keats and Wordsworth," he
contends, "have more soul, more reality of life than Shelley
has . . . . . And between these two poets Mr. Arnold's
choice is clearly Keats, Keats whose poetry caresses its own
beauty and moves to no other goal than its own vivid
flowering life."   This seems heretical.   Wordsworth is, by
Arnold's admission and by the general consent of his critics,
the principal influence on Arnold's poetry.   But how much

Arnold's lyrics, on really close inspection, do recall the peerless odes of Keats! Think of the stanzaic form of *Thyrsis* and *The Scholar Gipsy* and of the marked likeness in thought and feeling between the latter poem and the *Ode to a Nightingale*. Think of the constant crushing sense of death in the two poets and of their revulsion from the social life of their day. Think of their penchant to mirror the dramas of their personal life in ancient myths, and, in so doing, to bury the thought in elaborate decorative images. Of that fraction of Arnold's poetry which we can still read with delight, how much has the austere impress of Wordsworth, how much has the more sumptuous impress of Keats?

No less penetrating, and of certain validity, is a contrast which Louis Etienne draws between Arnold and Hazlitt.

"Mr. Matthew Arnold's pages on philistinism," he says, "recall those of Hazlitt on John Bull. . . . . Hazlitt was above all the critic of the individual's acumen. Better than any other critic he expressed the literary ideas which prevailed in England during the first third of the present century. . . . . He was a partisan and a man of passion. Matthew Arnold professes to be neither. Hazlitt was subject to his feelings. Matthew Arnold insists upon rules. Hazlitt abhorred the moderation which Matthew Arnold worships. Hazlitt was eminently English and used foreign things as foils merely to set off the excellence of English things. Matthew Arnold is cosmopolitan and to increase his strength in combat with the inert mass of the nation, he broadens the scope of his remarks and makes France, Germany and the ancient world his auxiliaries."

The contrast with Hazlitt was a deft device. No other English critic of anything like his stature would so well have illustrated how novel was Arnold's position and what large claims he might justly make upon the interest and the indulgence of a reader of the *Revue des deux mondes*. One is naturally led from this contrast to the question—is Arnold "an expatriated intelligence"? Louis Etienne happily and hospitably replies that "there is no better definition of Arnold's critical method than to say that it realizes our French ideas."

In July, 1864, a translation of Matthew Arnold's essay on Heine appeared in the *Revue Britannique*. A final note announced this essay as a sample of the prose of a modern English poet who was also a desultory contributor of prose to the English reviews and magazines; and promised a sample of his poetry—a promise never redeemed. In November, 1868, there appeared in the same review a translation and refutation of an article in *The Quarterly Review* in which Arnold's report on education in France had been assailed. The wisdom of Matthew Arnold's recommendations was adroitly upheld. In May, 1871, his essay on *The Literary Influence of Academies* appeared, shorn of some of its topical references likely to tax a foreign reader's attention; and in the preceding month an approximately complete version of *Pagan and Christian Religious Sentiment* had appeared.

Meanwhile Arnold's reputation was growing in those circles in France where English things were valued. Hippolyte Taine pressed him in the winter of 1864 to review his *Histoire de la littérature anglaise*. In very creditable French, Arnold thanked Taine for the honour done him and, in passing, for his treatment of Dr. Thomas Arnold in the history; but pleaded his preference for limited subjects and so begged off. In Odysse Barot's encyclopaedic *Histoire de la littérature contemporaine en Angleterre 1830-1874*, published in the latter year, Arnold figured in the honourable company of Leslie Stephen as "equally remarkable as poet, philosopher and publicist."

II. Critics of Arnold's Theological Adventures

Arnold's reputation in France was given a vigorous fillip by the publication of *Literature and Dogma*. In the midst of the *succès de scandale* which this book immediately achieved in England *The Academy* published on September 1, 1873, a review of it by a famous French orientalist, Albert Réville. This review is a model of that urbanity which Arnold was forever striving to import from France and which as his bugbears justly complained, he seldom attained in his own controversial prose. Réville begins by copious professions of modesty and salutes Arnold as a writer of European reputation who "passes on the continent as a writer of very great and very English originality which places him to some extent in a position of isolation even amongst his own countrymen." How neatly barbed the compliment is, how sure to wound deeply with a minimum of violence! Albert Réville pursues his attack with the same diabolic dexterity: "There is something in the combination of daring and moderation in his ideas, of tendencies often radical with conclusions generally conservative, that seems exactly fitted to bewilder a continental critic." Albert Réville was never less bewildered: he is simply out-Arnolding Matthew Arnold. After an elaborate analysis of the content of

Literature and Dogma he delivers, with unflagging charm an attack upon the impersonal nature of Arnold's god. "If the not ourselves which makes for righteousness" he protests, "is an unconscious force, I cannot feel for it that sacred emotion which raises morality to the rank of religion . . . . there will be no religion in my acquiescence . . . . I should only be able to feel towards the beneficent power, which was ignorant of its own existence something like the sentiment inspired by a mineral spring of which the waters have restored my failing health." This is piercing the weak joint in Arnold's armour: and if there were English critics who did so, no other performed the feat with Réville's surgical grace. The operation completed, Albert Réville withdraws, salving the wound with healing praise: "I have seldom read a book more penetrated with the great need that the present age feels for religious renovation, that, without breaking with the past will do justice to the progress accomplished by the general intelligence,"—the last phrase a wooden over-literal translation; and expresses a final hope, namely, "while maintaining my criticism, I sincerely wish and hope that England may send us many more books as powerfully conceived, as boldly written, as instructive and giving as much food for reflection, as this of Mr. Matthew Arnold." Little wonder that when *God and the Bible* appeared two years later *The Academy* again called upon Albert Réville for a review. Even on that strenuous and tedious book, he contrived a review, still lively to read, but never sacrificing soundness to eloquence or frippery. To almost every sentence in these two reviews, a modern reader can subscribe, delighting in their form and temper, accepting their content.

The *Revue Suisse*, that admirable organ of continental

liberal Protestantism, entrusted the review of *Literature and Dogma* to a regular contributor on philosophical and theological subjects, Charles Secrétan. His review, which appeared early in 1874, is jagged and uncouth when set beside the winning elegance of Albert Réville. In a few packed pages he resumes Arnold's argument,—a mistaken process, for the value of Arnold's work is atmospheric rather than dialectic. Secrétan's reaction to *Literature and Dogma*, to which Arnold's references in *God and the Bible* are unduly *simplistes*, is interesting. An intransigent Kantian, he resents Arnold's being neither fish nor flesh, neither a utilitarian like Seeley nor a Kantian like himself. He joins Arnold's English critics in deploring the tone of pleasantry which pervades even the holiest matter in the book—the assimilation of the popular conception of the Trinity to a trio of Shaftesburys. He joins them, too, in their reproach that Arnold treated what he very imperfectly understood and treated it in a pontifical manner. In compensation he does glad homage to Arnold's profound religious emotion and to the admirable positive and apologetic intention transparent in the work.

Secrétan and Albert Réville reviewed *Literature and Dogma* from its English edition. Alone of Arnold's books it had the honour of translation: in 1876, Germer-Ballière issued in their series *Bibliothèque de Philosophie Contemporaine* now published by Félix Alcan, a volume entitled *La Crise Religieuse*, a translation from the fifth edition of *Literature and Dogma*, corrected and revised by Matthew Arnold, and done by a Protestant army surgeon at that time in Algeria, one Sarazin, to whom Arnold frequently alludes in his domestic letters of that year. It is evident, also, from these letters that Arnold was extremely sensitive to the compliment implied in the translation of this work which, as late as 1883, he continued to regard as the most effective he had written.

The service that Sarazin rendered Arnold's foreign reputation was substantial. His translation was of use to a circle into which English books did not often penetrate. The French free-thinkers, attentive to all that dropped from the Gothic presses beyond the Rhine, expected little from across the channel. One of the wisest of these, Maurice Vernes, reviewed *La Crise Religieuse* in an elaborate article which he reprinted in 1880 under the title *Le Christianisme renouvelé d'après Arnold*, in his collection *Mélanges de critique religieuse*.

Although Maurice Vernes was doubtless unfamiliar with the articles of Albert Réville in *The Academy*, he adopted their method. "It is very easy to see," he says, "that only from an Englishman could such an effort come. . . . . This book is intensely national, stamped with the best qualities of the English mind, its clearness and its tenacity." The interest and the value of Maurice Vernes's examination of *Literature and Dogma* lies not so much in his evaluation of its argument as in his explanation of its historical significance. Ignorant, one supposes, of Cassel's anonymously published *Supernatural Religion*, he finds in *Literature and Dogma* "the first English effort to appropriate for English needs, the great critical labour of the Germans. "No other English book, he claims, "had accepted the results of this labour with so much sincerity and decision." Maurice Vernes then compares Arnold's intention with that of Von Hartmann's *The Religion of the Future*, and discovers in their contrast an illustration of the chasm between the German and the English mind. And, bent upon completeness, he also compares Arnold's attitude with that of the free-thinkers of France, engaged in constructing a moral system without obligation or sanction, an "independent ethic."

"The English writer," he suggests, "differs from his French analogues by his sense that the mass of moral beliefs required has been bequeathed by history in a complex, definitive and perfect form and that this bequest is happily lodged with the religion of his own nation in the Book which tradition designates as the strong-box of truth. . . . . What the free-thinkers of France have tried to determine by study of the mass of ideas on the moral activity of the individual commonly accepted to-day, Mr. Arnold, an Englishman and a Protestant, has tried to determine with the help of the tradition and customs of his people."

The upshot of Maurice Vernes's review is that if Arnold had not inherited a tenacious English reverence for the Bible, he would have vied with his French contemporaries in the erection of empirical moral systems. Maurice Vernes concedes that if "from a general point of view, from the point of view of humanity at large, *Literature and Dogma* is open to severe criticism, as a work destined for an English public it has a much superior value." If Maurice Vernes does not assume with Albert Réville that Matthew Arnold is a thinker or writer of European reputation but judges him rather as an example of specifically insular culture, nevertheless he does him the honour of scholarly attention and analysis, an honour few English critics deigned to do him.

One must beware of overestimating French interest in Arnold's books of religious criticism. No one in France would, I suppose, have been more likely to read them with curiosity than Ernest Renan. He was personally acquainted with Arnold; so close was the kinship of temperament between them that Arnold often spoke of it and that I have sometimes thought that Renan's *Souvenirs d'enfance et de jeunesse* was really the most illuminating book about the movement of Arnold's mind that I have ever read. Arnold sent all his works of religious criticism to Renan, with gracious dedications; and on Renan's death they passed with most of his other books to the Bibliothèque Nationale, where they now form a part of the Renan Collection. When I had them in my hands in the winter of 1928, I noticed that neither Renan nor anyone else had cared to cut more than a few pages of any volume.

III. LATER JUDGMENTS

We may now leave these high but somewhat dull matters, and note in 1881, in the first study in the seventh series of Edmond Schérer's *Etudes sur la littérature contemporaine*, an account of Arnold's manifold literary activities that went to Arnold's heart. "Schérer," he wrote to his Huguenot correspondent Fontanès, "was very good and very just— and his compliment to myself charming." He had just published his collection of *Mixed Essays*, in which he had chosen Schérer as his guide in revisiting Milton and Goethe. Schérer was returning the "compliment" by a choice of Matthew Arnold's anthology of Wordsworth's poetry, published in 1879, as the focus of a presentation of that poet to the French public. No other compliment, except perhaps one to his father, could have pleased Arnold so exquisitely; and Schérer, much more effusive to Arnold than Arnold to Schérer, embroidered it with a breathless succession of superlatives. Matthew Arnold appears before the French public as a prodigious amalgam of theological lore, critical acumen and lyric inspiration; he is a singular example of unlimited curiosity; he is a writer who has excelled in every mode of expression he has essayed; he is "the most lively, the most fastidious, the most elegant of critics, the critic who has put in circulation the greatest number of ideas, who has given these ideas their most piquant formulation, whose combination of audacity and sense has most efficaciously prodded the inertness of English thought."

It is evident that Schérer's intention is more complimentary than analytical. Certain of his *obiter dicta*, however, deserve examination. He insists upon Arnold's versatility in poetry, upon his force and charm in the lyric, epic, and dramatic modes, upon the peculiar "savour" of his elegies and upon the grandeur of his reflective poetry. And he concludes that "the poetic idiom has rarely voiced a thought which so unites breadth of range and clearness of articulation." Now almost any critic to whom Victorian tendencies in feeling and thinking are not generically repellent, will admit that Arnold's poetry has intensity and a rare measure of articulation. But no one to-day would contend for its versatility. The "absolutely personal stamp" to which Schérer elsewhere alludes is what gives it its charm and its power, a stamp so personal as to preclude even the expectation of versatility. This questionable opinion of Arnold's versatility also invades Schérer's description of his criticism and leads the Swiss critic to claim that Arnold "can never be surprised in a dogmatic attitude or in a pretentious phrase." And Schérer continues: "How refreshing it is to open his books when one has just been reading great but mannered writers. . . . . Carlyle with his deliberate jargon, Ruskin with his affectation of depth, his laborious effort to be striking." One might almost reverse Schérer's judgment, find spontaneity in the incoherence of Carlyle and the torrential flow of Ruskin, find pretence and artifice in the limpid, very careful sentences of Arnold. It is not difficult, however, to explain Schérer's attitude: for a Frenchman of 1880, to conform was to avoid, not to invite, artifice. Artifice was in the undue assertion of individuality. The elements of French civilization which Arnold had absorbed stand him in good stead with Schérer, who exclaims: "There is a kind of ingratitdue in the ignorance in which we remain of Mr. Arnold's works; for there is no foreign writer better posted on the literature of France, more sympathetic, I was going to say more indulgent, to our cast of mind, our society, our institutions." It is worth pointing out the apparent antinomy between the conception of Arnold's cosmopolitanism common to Schérer and the critics of the *Revue des deux mondes* and the conception of his insularity emphatically affirmed by Albert Réville and Maurice Vernes.

After his protracted compliment to his guide, Schérer undertakes the exploration of Wordsworth's poetry; and thereafter Arnold is but an incidental reference. In taking leave of Wordsworth, however, Schérer utters a prophecy that time has verified. "I should not be surprised," he says, "if the anthology of his poetry published by Mr. Matthew Arnold and the attention thus drawn to him would avail to fix his final place in the galaxy of British genius." Few critical works have been so effective as

Arnold's volume of Wordsworth—as even Professor Lane Cooper, inclined to carp at its preface and selections alike, has conceded.

In the early eighties Matthew Arnold's utterances on questions of the day were chronicled by the *Revue Suisse* and always given a favourable evaluation. His papers in *The Nineteenth Century* for April and June, 1881, the papers in which he proposed ungrudging admission that Ireland had been gravely wronged and merited reparation, were reported at some length under the rubric *Chronique Anglaise.* The chronicler says, inspired by the penitent temper of these papers: "One must in justice admit that despite their national pride, the English do not spare themselves the statement of unpleasant truths. This virtue they owe to their Protestant religion and to their habitual practice of examining their consciences." In 1882, Arnold's Rede Lecture at Cambridge on the inviting theme *Literature and Science*, was reported in remarkable detail and with perfect accuracy. The brief comment of the chronicler is conceived in words of fervid admiration.

In 1885, the publication of *Discourses in America* prompted Léo Quesnel, a prolific contributor to the *Revue Suisse*, to write a general article on Matthew Arnold's works and his rank in current literature. The article, *Un Moraliste Anglais*, begins with an auspicious compliment which recalls Arnold's own manner in introducing his foreign favourites: "Any utterance of Mr. Matthew Arnold's, whether spoken or written, whether in a paper, a lecture or a book, is always a literary event." After a brief excursus upon the recent *Discourses in America*, the pretext rather than the matter of his article, he accounts for the perhaps extravagant eulogy of his opening sentence, saying:

"It is because he is passionately zealous in his worship of truth, because he represents in our age the spirit consecrated to criticism, the critical spirit in its loftiest degree. .... He is the Emerson, the Renan of England: like them, indeed, he is subject to criticism, subject to blame, but like them he compels a hearing and applause."

These are words exquisitely chosen to delight Matthew Arnold: they express the function that he strove to fulfil and they compare his fulfilment of it with that of two of the very few contemporaries for whom he had an almost zealous respect.

What Léo Quesnel has to say of Arnold's poetry excites wonder. Of parts of this poetry he has a very high opinion, although he rejects quite summarily the claim advanced by some English critics that Arnold's rank is the first in contemporary English poetry. But what he chiefly, almost exclusively, admires in Arnold's poetry are his sonnets and his epic fragments, his epic fragments more than his sonnets. Among the epic fragments he singles out, of all things, *Balder Dead*, (neglecting *Tristan and Iseult*, neglecting *Sohrab and Rustum*), for quotation and comment. "*Balder Dead* will remain," says this curious reviewer, "his title to glory." Even within the chosen limits of his favourite poem, Léo Quesnel's judgment works strangely. One must, I think, be a determined admirer of Matthew Arnold to discover charm in *Balder Dead*. But if the poem have charm, surely that charm is in the passages where Balder's character is revealed and Arnold's quiet liking for him as a kindred child of light, a being naturally tender, bright and beautiful. Léo Quesnel admires and quotes passages descriptive merely of the primitive setting, against which

Arnold defines the essentially modern character of Balder. It is difficult to suppose that any careful reader of *Sohrab and Rustum* and *Balder Dead* would prefer the austere nature traced in fine outline in *Balder Dead* to the sumptuous Oriental magnificence of the natural and martial background in *Sohrab and Rustum*. Two alternative suggestions present themselves. Perhaps Léo Quesnel's mastery of English may have been modest, in which event *Sohrab and Rustum*, by its wealth of concrete language and by its Miltonic complication of syntax, may have been too much for him. Or his taste was frigidly classical.

This latter suggestion is inadmissible. He says: "The characters in Mr. Arnold's poetry, (and perhaps even that poetry itself), have been likened to a gallery of Greek marble statuary; this is beyond doubt high praise: but for us, men of the nineteenth century, this praise is almost a reproach." In amplification of this narrowly modern attitude he observes of Arnold's poetry in general that it has no appeal for the ordinary reader "who in every age has looked, in poetry, only for the expression of thoughts and feelings that he has himself experienced." Léo Quesnel, then, chooses as Arnold's masterpiece the one among his poems which is most remote from modern thought and feeling; and turns upon Arnold's poetry as a whole with the reproach of remoteness! Ignorance is the only explanation of such an error.

And, indeed, Léo Quesnel hastily despatches Arnold's poetry to come to his genuine interest, Arnold's prose. His knowledge and justice in the latter part of his paper are equally admirable. The gospel of sweetness and light with its "implications of universal insight and universal charity," the doctrine of the grand style with its political analogues in aristocratic society, the campaign for French methods in English education,—these are touched on briefly but with precision and regard. From Arnold's more ambitious efforts, from his scheme of social philosophy, from his Biblical exegesis, Léo Quesnel turns away, prudently saying that to sift these too closely would be unjust. "Arnold," he says, "as it is easy to see, is less an adept in these empirical sciences than a man of feeling, of inspiration, of charity." In conclusion Léo Quesnel offers an analysis and a criticism of the American discourse on *Numbers*. The sagacity of Arnold's fears for democracy, of his attachment to authority, the Swiss critic concedes; but he regrets that a liberal mind like Arnold's, a mind committed to belief in the regenerative value of public education and national culture, should be the victim of these fears. In another happy observation he opposes Arnold's attitude to the *Zeitgeist*, and suggests that Arnold has placed himself in fatal opposition to the "irresistible current" which had long been his practical criterion of value. The defect of the discourse on *Numbers*, its fundamental assumption that the sins of an exaggerated democracy, an ochlocracy, are inseparable from any democratic society, is excellently set forth. But whatever one may say of the matter of *Numbers*, its artistic perfection is, as Léo Quesnel adds, unquestionable. "Mr. Arnold has chosen the lecture as his medium, the medium of a master of conversation. Such a master is a rarity in England. But Mr. Arnold has lived in the society of Frenchmen, and he combines in his character the Germanic seriousness and the Gallic swiftness of perception."

The next French notice of Matthew Arnold came from one of the contemporary free-thinkers with whose schemes of society Maurice Vernes had compared his, J.-M. Guyau.

In his vivacious widely-read and still readable venture into social philosophy, *L'Irreligion de l'Avenir*, he impugned the unduly simplified conspectus of Western history in *Literature and Dogma*. His resentment was probably prompted by the almost Pecksniffian tone in which Arnold published to a complacent race the moral turpitude of their French neighbours and implied that the catastrophic years of 1870 and 1871 were a natural retribution for this, and an experimental proof of the invalidity of the French ideal of integral living. "The world, thinks Mr. Matthew Arnold, was judged in 1870: the Prussians filled the role of Jehovah. The spirit of Greece, the spirit of France, the spirit of the Renaissance, Free-Thought and Free-Love, were defeated by Israël, the Biblical spirit, the spirit of the Middle Ages. . . . . Jehovah is still the God of armies: and cursed be the people, cursed be the individuals who do not believe, with the Hebrews, that renunciation is three-fourths of life, and art and science but the remaining fourth." The caustic tone of Guyau, his undue simplification of Matthew Arnold's thought which is more an atmosphere than a logical concatenation, must not prejudice for us the point of his criticism. No idealist can defer to the incidental judgments of historical processes, and no historian will lightly attempt to fix their moral purport; and Guyau was both idealist and historian. Further, the antiquated sort of typology in which Arnold freely indulges, defining the function of an almost immemorial society in a breezy deft phrase, obscures what measure of truth there may be at the base of Arnold's generalizations. It prevents Guyau, for example, from seeing any truth whatever in Arnold's deplorably clerical assimilation of the French ideal to the ideal of *l'homme sensuel moyen*. Now Matthew Arnold was an indefatigable and meticulous observer of social facts; he understood French life and literature (so Sainte Beuve's compliment went), as a foreign country may be understood only by one who has a peculiar personal affinity with it; and when he concentrated his opinion of French life and literature in one telling phrase, this phrase would not be the mere pulpit-thunder that it seemed to Guyau. The phrase is wildly sensational but it conceals (rather than reveals, one must admit) a considerable meaning. Paris, he always admitted, is the capital of intelligence and taste; it is humanism at its fullest development, the world at its best. Nevertheless it has the defects of its qualities, it is still worldly, still human, still below the civic ideal of the eldest son of Dr. Thomas Arnold.

Elsewhere in his book, Guyau examines the theological and moral substance of *Literature and Dogma*, which he appears to have studied in the original. With a pleasant and somewhat unexpected delicacy of statement, he suggests that Arnold stands on the verge of the agnostic abyss and that the cords which secure his belief in the tradition of his nurture are the slenderest yet seen. He insists, rightly, upon the remoteness of Arnold's doctrine, in which religious events are treasured merely for their symbolic and aesthetic virtue, from any doctrine ever held by a Christian collectivity. And in a striking phrase he defines Arnold as the defender not of a religion but simply of a human ethic with religious sanctions. The radical difference between English and Latin minds appears in Guyau's complaint,—a complaint in which he echoes, perhaps unconsciously, the Italian critic Angelo di Gubernatis writing some years before in the *Nuova Antologia*,—that the ethic in question is defaced rather than supported by these sanctions. "Can Mr. Arnold fail to see," Guyau inquires, "that if the real is, as he himself says, supremely great and beautiful, then we have no longer any need of the legendary, even when it is interpreted after Mr. Arnold's fashion: the real world,—in which I include the world of moral, as well as the world of physical reality,—is altogether sufficient to our thought." This leaves no more to be said.

The *Revue Suisse* returned twice again to the subject of Arnold. On the occasion of his death in April, 1888, in its English chronicle, a complete and generous necrology appeared. The appeal of his poetry to the literary circles of London and their conviction that Arnold's principal achievement was in poetry; his own preference for his theological propaganda; the chronicler's obligation to the prophet of the social gospel of sweetness and light; his laborious life as an inspector and the decisive influence of his reports on continental education; in short, all the public aspects of Arnold's life, are touched on with a competent and graceful hand. The account of his activity justifies the chronicler's claim that "no man in our time has moved in more of the currents of English life; and he has never failed to win the regard of even his adversaries." In 1896, the English chronicler of the review paid a final homage to Arnold, in a mention of G. W. E. Russell's edition of Arnold's letters.

In 1894, M. Max Leclerc, who never wearies of travelling, published a critical account of a year spent in observation of English secondary instruction, *L'éducation des classes moyennes et dirigeantes en Angleterre*. In the opinion of M. Leclerc, Matthew Arnold is the ideal guide for such studies as his,—a guide with exhaustive knowledge of the actual state of English secondary instruction and articulate conceptions of the improvements it required. His name recurs again and again; and the tone of trust in which it is uttered appears to deepen as the study proceeds, until M. Leclerc's final suggestions for the organization of secondary instruction are conscious echoes and amplifications of Arnold's.

IV. Excursus: Swiss Critics

In 1904 appeared at Basle, and in English, a thesis by A. Schrag on *Matthew Arnold, Poet and Critic*. Commonplace in its general ideas, eccentric in its taste, stodgy in its style, defective in its knowledge of Arnold, this is the worst work —or was, until Mr. Hugh Kingsmill's appeared two years ago—that Arnold has occasioned. Mr. Schrag informs us that Clough achieved better rhythm in his poetry than Arnold,—a judgment which Fraülein Lutonsky reverses in her study of Clough, and which, indeed, clamours for correction; he warns us that none of Arnold's poems "not one single poem"—"flows from the heart like a natural spring"; he identifies Arnold with "the classical school of the eighteenth century,"—an indefensible assimilation which is not improved by the choice of Gray, a nostalgic pre-romantic, as the type of this school; strangest of all Mr. Schrag's aberrations are his complacent assertions that "pessimism" and "ethics" are irreconcilable, that the sole poetry for future generations will be "ethical," and that the pessimistic poetry of Arnold will therefore lose the siren's appeal that it had for contemporaries. One wonders what poets Mr. Schrag read and where he acquired his delimitations of poetry!

The Swiss, it is sad to say, have betrayed an unfortunate obstinacy in writing wretched books on Matthew Arnold,

whereas throughout his life he honoured their country with
an unwavering affection; the only *books* which come within
the purview of this study are Swiss. In 1910, M. Georges
Poisblaud, a Swiss Calvinist pastor who had for some years
held a Lowland Scottish charge, presented as a bacca-
laureate thesis at Geneva a study of *La Religion fondée sur
le vérifiable d'après Matthew Arnold*. This is a sermon,
packed with hollow rhetoric, rather than a thesis. The
inadequacy of M. Poisblaud's knowledge is shown in his
appreciation of Arnold's style: "Matthew Arnold wrote
rapidly; therefore the same sentences, the same definitions
are perpetually returning, often with wearing effect." Now
M. Poisblaud was using the French translation of *Literature
and Dogma*; and this translation had been based upon the
fifth edition in book-form of *Literature and Dogma*; and
this edition had benefited by four previous revisions of the
text as well as by the revision undertaken for it. The
ascription of the peculiarities in the text to haste in composition is an unpleasant evidence of haste in conjecture.
Conjecture and rhetoric are the staples of this book. In
the first chapter M. Poisblaud sketches the life and work of
Arnold, making the rare facts mentioned pegs for moral
aberrations. Arnold, he tells us, was always a poet, a man
of impulse, crying out what he feels, an *enfant terrible* for
whom serious philosophical reasoning was too grave an
occupation. One must excuse the feebleness of Arnold's
arguments, and their occasional naïveté, for in his peculiar
rambling "he strews rare pearls and authentic jewels."
The above paraphrase of one of M. Poisblaud's flights
reveals the tawdry pinch-beck nature of his book. In a
second chapter, equally objectionable, the style and the
polemical intention of Arnold are considered; and in a

third and fourth chapter, the experimental method of *Literature and Dogma* is analysed and its validity criticised. These chapters are as disappointing in content and method as in tone: the later theological works of Arnold, the articles of contemporary critics, English, French, Swiss and Dutch, and, especially the articles of Rauwenhoff in the *Theological Review* of Leyden, should have been M. Poisblaud's auxiliaries in his exegesis,—and he fails to mention one of them. To Arnold's faith in the known and the knowable he opposes a faith in the unknown and the unknowable; against Arnold's preference, in the decisive matter of religion, for the patient perfectible methods of experience, he sets up his personal preference for the uncertain and incorrigible method of intuition. He confounds his pedestrian contrast of these two methods with a refutation of the experimental method of Matthew Arnold.   Stripped of its not very deceptive garb of pulpit-rhetoric, this is the substance of M. Poisblaud's thesis; and one questions whether if Arnold had lived to read it he might not have retracted his compliment to Geneva "that home of large instruction and lucid intelligence."

V. POSTHUMOUS REPUTATION

Matthew Arnold's posthumous reputation in France has been chiefly and almost exclusively among academic specialists, among the highly competent corps of *anglicistes* who man the seventeen national universities.   But what they have said of Arnold is not, with one important exception, to our purpose, for their outlook upon English literature is not national but special,—the outlook of an international guild. Take, for example, the able summary of Arnold's contribution to the intellectual development of Victorianism in M. Charles Cestre's war-time synthesis, *France, England and America.* There is scarcely a single detail of interpretation in it to distinguish it from the contemporaneous study of Stuart Sherman. Or take M. Louis Cazamian's chapters on Arnold in his *Modern England* or in his second volume of the *History of English Literature.* Addressed to a more academic audience than M. Cestre was seeking they reveal a greater complexity of exposition and evaluation; but even more patently they are the achievement of a mind fastidiously free from all merely national traits. And so with other minor studies of which I shall mention only M. Louis Bonnerot's detective work upon Arnold's love-poetry in the *Revue anglo-américaine* for August, 1930. M. Bonnerot puts the suspicion in our breast that he may some day add a companion brochure to M. Legouis's study of Wordsworth's French daughter.*

The single exception that I reserved the right to treat is M. Legouis's reconsideration of Arnold's judgment on French poetry. In 1911, in London and later in Oxford, M. Legouis delivered in four lectures a *Défense de la poésie française à l'usage des lecteurs anglais.* "Matthew Arnold," he says, "was foremost in my mind when I chose as the subject of these lectures a defence of French poetry." Why Matthew Arnold, rather than De Quincey or Carlyle, who have said far more fatuous things of French poetry than Arnold ever did? Because these other authors were so evidently eccentric in their judgments of French literature

---

*While this study was passing through the press M. Charles Cestre kindly informed me that among the *Sept études de littérature anglaise* of M. Paul Chauvet (Paris, Figuière, 1931) there is an essay on the poetry of Matthew Arnold.

that an American or Englishman who has made the first
step toward an understanding of France will heed them no
more than he would the nearest maniac in the nearest
asylum. Unfortunately, as M. Legouis long ago discovered, he will heed and continue to heed Matthew Arnold.
For Matthew Arnold understood France better than any
of his English-speaking contemporaries and, with the exception of W. C. Brownell and Barrett Wendell, better than
any of his successors. And for more than half a century, as
I have pointed out in the course of this paper, French critics
of the clearest intelligence, agreeing with Villemain, have
conceded that he understood France perfectly. He was a
courier of French conceptions; and yet, in M. Legouis's
phrase, this ally was in a matter of the greatest moment an
adversary. "And that," to quote again, "is the more
painful since Arnold was a poet, very nearly a great poet,
and a man who firmly believed that poetry was the highest
expression of the human spirit."

With a dialectic and an urbanity finer than Arnold's
own, M. Legouis establishes the silliness of the verse

"France, famed in all great arts, in none supreme,"

from one of Arnold's early sonnets, and the unscrupulous
cunning with which in his essay on Heine he chose quotations which were to "represent" French poetry and suggest
its tunelessness and hollow rhetoric. It is certain that
Arnold was quite impervious to French poetry; but one is
just as uncertain after a study of M. Legouis's lectures as
when one came to them, why he should have been impervious. He appears to have had a cultivated ear for Italian
poetry; he wrote French with felicity and was remarkably

sensitive to the music of French prose, ancient and modern. I venture to suggest that his failure with French poetry is closely allied to his equally abject failure with English poetry from Dryden to Johnson. I can imagine no worse preparation for a study of French poetry than a conviction that Dryden and Pope are merely "classics of our prose."

Aside from the French professors of English literature, Arnold has lately found at least one eager French reader, through whose mediation his conception of the poetic experience has played a part in the principal literary controversy of the past decade,—the debate on pure poetry beween M. Paul Souday and the Abbé Henri Brémond. Led to read Arnold by Schérer's eulogy, the Abbé Brémond draws upon him as one of the mere handful of critics who have understood what poetry is and what it does. The Abbé Brémond quotes extensively from Arnold; but the crucial passage for him, a passage too little remembered by English critics, consists of two sentences:

"The grand power of poetry is its interpretative power; by which I mean, not a power of drawing out in black and white an explanation of the mystery of the universe, but the power of so dealing with things as to awaken in us a wonderfully full, new and intimate sense of them and of our relations with them. When this sense is awakened in us, as to objects without us, we feel ourselves to be in contact with the essential nature of those objects, to be no longer bewildered and oppressed by them but to have their secret, and to be in harmony with them; and this feeling calms and satisfies us as no other can."

This, from the essay on *Maurice de Guérin*, is Arnold's ablest statement of his esoteric doctrine of poetry; and it is a thousand pities that not only the casual critics but the convinced Arnoldians as well should continue to identify him with such clap-trap catchwords as "a criticism of life" and "a consolation and a stay."

I do not suppose that it was the reading of Arnold that moulded the Abbé Brémond's conception of poetry; literary influences do not operate with such brutality upon minds of his magnitude. I do suggest that in Arnold the Abbé Brémond found one of the most impressive corroborations of his conception; and I believe that to a close reader of *Prière et Poésie* the conviction will come that for the Abbé's bridge between the religious and the aesthetic experience, the doctrine of Arnold was a great deal more than a decorative excrescence.

The French reputation of Matthew Arnold, in its meagreness, illustrates the law that "what one people seeks in the culture of another is not the reflection of its own genius but the impact of something evidently alien." It was a matter of the greatest moment to Matthew Arnold and to the England of his age that he had a deep affinity with the spirit of France. To France it was a matter of no moment whatever. The only one of his books that the French cared to translate, the only one that stirred more than a few French minds to excitement, was the most eccentric, the most erratic, the most provincial of them all, —*Literature and Dogma*. The French reputation of Arnold is a negative illustration of another law. When a writer achieves a widespread influence abroad, when in some measure he shapes the course of a foreign thought or literature, his success is normally purchased at the cost of deformation. He is praised for the wrong things. To read Gundolf's study of *Shakespeare und der deutsche Geist,* or to investigate the mythical reputation of Macchiavelli in France and England is to be convinced of this. Arnold was never influential enough in France to undergo such a deformation; his French reputation is as sound as it is slight; and its very soundness proves its slightness.

———